D1395123

ADMIRAL SIR WILLIAM FISHER

Books by Sir William James

THE BRITISH NAVY IN ADVERSITY
(A Study of the War of American Independence)

BLUE WATER AND GREEN FIELDS

COMMANDER-IN-CHIEF, MEDITERRANEAN

ADMIRAL SIR WILLIAM FISHER

BY

ADMIRAL SIR WILLIAM JAMES

LONDON
MACMILLAN & CO. LTD
1943

First Edition October 1943
Reprinted October 1943

PRINTED IN GREAT BRITAIN
BY R. & R. CLARK, LIMITED, EDINBURGH

To

THE OFFICERS AND MEN OF THE ROYAL NAVY

whose efficiency and high courage in the Second World War would have been a source of pride to him who, throughout his career, set the highest standard of conduct and service and laboured unremittingly to prepare the Fleet for the supreme test he knew lay ahead

CONTENTS

LIST OF ILLUSTRATIONS

INTRODUCTION

In the long and colourful history of the Royal Navy no earlier period was so vivid and eventful as that between 1901 and 1918. In those few years the Royal Navy underwent a complete transformation in types of ships and, consequently, in tactical methods, and, when transformed, was put to the severest test in its history during a four-years war whose outcome was in the balance until the end.

In 1901 the Fleet consisted of slow, coal-burning battleships and cruisers, and a few destroyers ; the submarine was still in the experimental stage. The efficiency of main armaments was tested annually at a range of about 2000 yards ; torpedoes ran for about 800 yards.

By 1914 the Fleet consisted of fast, oil-burning, all-big-gun battleships and battle cruisers whose main armaments could engage an enemy at 20,000 yards, and over a hundred destroyers whose torpedoes could run straight for about 8000 yards ; the submarine had become a weapon of such potency that many believed it would dominate in maritime war, and naval officers and designers were already turning their thoughts to a ship that could carry aircraft and accompany the Fleet. It was a dynamic period, and never before had officers and men worked so hard in peace-time to produce and perfect a Fleet that would be ready for its historic task of controlling the sea lines of communication in the event of war. To the determination that the Royal Navy must never drop from its proud position as the first navy in the world was added the certainty that the Kaiser would challenge our sea supremacy as soon as he had built up his fleet to commensurate proportions.

The years before the outbreak of the First World War

were thus years of great opportunity for officers of vision, who were also leaders of men; robust, wise leadership was at a premium when there was so much to be done, and done quickly. Amongst the hundreds of officers striving to develop the new weapons and to increase all-round efficiency, W. W. Fisher stood out, because of his striking personality, fine presence, clear-thinking brain, and gift of drawing whole-hearted service from officers and men who came in contact with him. Like many other distinguished officers, he was denied the opportunity of taking a prominent part in naval battle because, on the only occasion the British and German battle fleets were in contact, the German Commander-in-Chief's sole object was to avoid battle, and this he could do as his ships were as fast as those of his opponent, and the visibility often decreased to a few miles during those tense hours off Jutland. But if the High Sea Fleet was not to be risked, no such defeatist policy governed the German submarine campaign which, at the time of Jutland, was growing in intensity and causing grave forebodings to those of our statesmen and sailors who knew the facts of the sinkings and the enemy submarine output. There might never be another meeting of the two main fleets, but, unless we could counter the activities of the submarines more effectively, we might soon lose the war through destruction of our shipping. Faced with this serious situation, the Government decided to ask Lord Jellicoe to come to the Admiralty and cope with the menace, and he chose Fisher for the key appointment of Director of Anti-submarine Warfare. To this vitally important task Fisher brought his vision, immense energy, and high professional knowledge, and, as all the world knows, the menace was slowly and steadily reduced to acceptable proportions. No naval officer now doubted that Fisher would rise rapidly to the head of his profession.

Peace brought the inevitable reduction of the Fleet

and slowing-up of weapon development, but Fisher was on two occasions holding responsible appointments when war clouds were gathering. He was Chief of the Staff to the Commander-in-Chief in the Mediterranean during the Russian Civil War and the long months of strained relations with Turkey, and he was Commander-in-Chief in the Mediterranean during those highly charged months when, owing to Mussolini's ambition to found a twentieth-century Roman Empire, there was a possibility that we, though deserted by many signatories of the League Covenant, would honour our signature and stop Italy's advance into Africa by force. A young officer in one of his ships expressed the feeling of every officer and man in the fleet: "We in the Mediterranean Fleet thanked God that W. W. Fisher was our Commander-in-Chief."

Fisher's sudden and unexpected death when holding the appointment of Commander-in-Chief, Portsmouth, was a very severe loss to the country and the Navy. The Service regarded him as the rightful successor to Lord Chatfield, and as First Sea Lord he would have enjoyed the full confidence of officers and men, would have undoubtedly held office with great dignity and distinction, and would have been a tower of strength at the council table when Ministers and their professional advisers were faced with a steadily deteriorating situation after the Germans marched into Norway. But, though that was not to be, the Navy, when once more called on to fight, knew how much they owed to W. W. Fisher for his inspiring leadership and unremitting efforts to train the Fleet for war during the years when appeasement and disarmament were the watchwords of all politicians in power except two, Hitler and Mussolini. He had all the gifts that heredity can bestow. He had a presence that can only be described as magnificent, coupled with a brain and a personality that would have taken him to the highest rank of any profession. His interests and enthusiasms were not confined to his profession. Anything beautiful — a picture, music, architecture — always stirred his senses, and his vivid and colourful descriptions of countryside or scenery, some of which are quoted in this book, show how deeply he was moved by the wonders and beauties of nature. He loved the smell of woods and fields and his quick eye missed nothing — not a tree or a bird or an animal — when he was striding over the rough Mediterranean uplands or through English lanes. He loved youth and he was always young. During his fifty years of service he gave unstintingly of everything that was in him ; so much did he give that he died many years before his time.

I undertook to write this life-story of a distinguished gentleman and great sailor at the request of Lady Fisher, because, like most of my contemporaries, I feel that the names of those primarily responsible for the battle-worthiness of the Royal Navy, when Germany for the second time set out to dominate the world, should not be forgotten, but should be held in high honour by their countrymen. I bring very little experience to the task, and Fisher's strong personality and character would be far more fittingly presented to the public by one of his many friends of literary distinction. But since any record of a sailor's life must include many references to his highly specialised work afloat, which is a closed book to those who have not served in the Fleet, Lady Fisher felt that a true record to be given to the Navy could only be written by a naval officer who had lived through the same times. Some references to the history of the period covered by this book are necessary to provide the setting in which Fisher worked, but I have kept these to a minimum, as it is "W. W", as he was known to thousands of officers and men, whose portrait I have endeavoured to draw.

W. M. J.

Road Farm, Churt
Dec. 1942

CHAPTER I

1875-1890

Early Days — Lynam's, Oxford — H.M.S. *Britannia*

WILLIAM WORDSWORTH FISHER was born on the 26th March, 1875. His father was Herbert William Fisher, son of the Rev. William Fisher, a Canon of Salisbury. He acted for a short time as tutor to the Prince of Wales, afterwards King Edward VII, at Oxford and Cambridge, and was afterwards Private Secretary to the Duke of Newcastle during the Crimean War, and from 1863 to 1870 acted as Private Secretary and Comptroller to the Prince of Wales. The Prince of Wales was devoted to him and was very angry when he expressed a wish to give up the appointment. He had never liked Court life and longed to settle in the country. In 1870 he was appointed Vice-Warden of the Stannaries, a Court dating back from the reign of King John, to deal with litigation relating to the mines in Cornwall and Devon. Fisher's mother was the daughter of John Jackson, for many years the leading physician in Calcutta, and Maria Pattle, who was one of seven remarkable sisters, of whom perhaps Mrs. Julia Cameron, the pioneer in artistic photography, Mrs. Prinsep, who for many years was a well-known London hostess at Little Holland House and the early patroness of G. F. Watts, and Lady Somers were the most conspicuous. The eldest sister, Adeline, married Halford Vaughan, sometime Regius Professor of Modern History at Oxford. The youngest, Julia, married Leslie Stephen ; Virginia Woolf, the novelist, and Vanessa Bell, the artist, were the offspring of this marriage.

Mrs. Fisher's great-grandfather was the Chevalier de L'Etang, page to Marie Antoinette, from whom sprang the exceptionally good looks of the family. She was a remarkable woman and an inspiration to her large family. The following is an extract from a short notice that appeared in *The Times* when she was killed by a motor car when crossing a London street :

> Of a rare beauty, utterly selfless, and gifted with extraordinary force and purity of character, Mrs. Fisher was an inspiration to everyone who knew her. Age and sorrow could not dim her radiant and heroic spirit. She was quick, vehement and gentle, frail but untiring, and of instantaneous judgment. She gave to all who came to her for comfort nothing less than her entire heart.

William, whose second name derived from the poet, a first cousin of his grandfather's, came eighth in a family of eleven gifted children. His eldest sister married F. W. M. Maitland, Downing Professor of Law at Cambridge, and after his death, Sir Francis Darwin, youngest son of Charles Darwin. His sister Emmeline married R. O. Morris, a Professor at the Royal College of Music, and his third sister, Adeline, married Dr. Ralph Vaughan Williams, O.M. His eldest brother, H. A. L. Fisher, was the eminent historian, a Cabinet Minister and Warden of New College, Oxford. Another brother, Charles Dennis, who was in character most like him, was a much-beloved and inspiring tutor at Christ Church, and was lost in the *Invincible* at Jutland when serving as a Lieutenant R.N.V.R. The youngest of the family, Edwin Fisher, became Chairman of Barclays Bank.

The Fishers were a most devoted family and, though William was parted from his brothers and sisters for four years very early in life and was in his subsequent sea career often abroad for long periods, he always kept in close touch with them and their affairs.

Brought up in such gifted company, he acquired more

general knowledge than most boys of his age and developed early a love of the Classics, which stood him in good stead when the time came for him to go to school and which he never lost, though the Classics were not included in naval education at any stage. When Commander-in-Chief, Mediterranean, he kept up a correspondence in Latin with a Jugoslav Professor with whom he had struck up a friendship at Split.

His father had been left a lovely house near Brockenhurst; and it was in the perfect surroundings of the New Forest that William spent his early years. It was an ideal life for young people. They hunted or ran with the hounds and acquired a love of nature and wild life that held them in thrall for the rest of their lives. In after life William often talked of the wonderful lessons his father and mother gave him and of how his father had such a sensitive ear that he could not bear his classical "floaters", and that, rather than lose his temper, he would rush out and talk to the horses in the stable and come back restored. When old enough, William was sent to Lynam's at Oxford. He was not long there before he was moved up to the Upper Sixth on account of his proficiency in Greek, and he found no difficulty in answering French examination papers. In one letter home he is looking forward with some apprehension to writing a Latin essay on Cromwell and, in another, he writes that he has done fairly well in a History paper in which he had to discuss "The Divine Right of Kings" and write short accounts of the lives of two of Charles I's supporters.

It is evident that he shared with his brothers high intellectual qualities inherited from gifted parents and, if he had not chosen the Navy for his profession, he would probably have been a distinguished scholar or historian.

The Navy was his own choice. Biographers of famous sea captains are always at pains to discover why their hero at a very early age persuaded his parents to allow him to go to sea. Sometimes the boy's home was near a Royal Dockyard and his mind was made up as soon as he could walk and talk. A full-rigged ship tacking up the narrows would fire the imagination of the dullest-witted boy and an occasional visit to the dockyard, where some ships would be fitting out for foreign service and others were being warped into dock to the shrill calls of the boatswains' pipes and bustling activity of hundreds of sailors, would steel his determination to wear the King's uniform. In other cases the boy's imagination was fired by listening to stories of service at sea in peace and war told by relatives or friends, who visited his home. Neither of these influences was present in young Fisher's case. He was a delicate, sensitive boy and not cut out then for the rough-and-tumble of life at sea. He was within three weeks of going up for a Winchester Scholarship when his father received a nomination for a cadetship and, though his parents had some doubts if he was physically and temperamentally fitted for a sea life, they wrote and gave him the chance. He replied in no uncertain terms that he wished to join the Navy :—

I have just received your letter and I should be very glad if you would accept the nomination — I have been waiting to hear what you thought upon the matter eagerly and am very glad indeed to hear its issue. Please excuse pencil and this short note — I will write a longer one tomorrow but shall not change my opinion.

He took the examination in September, 1888.

The Navy that young Fisher was about to enter was approaching the end of the " Groping Age ". Ever since the steam-engine had been adapted to move ships by paddle or screw propeller, designers and naval officers of all maritime nations had been groping to produce a ship that would steam fast, provide a steady gun platform in a rough sea, be adequately protected by armour against the shells of enemy ships of similar design and be able to remain at sea for long periods.

The *Britannia*, which Fisher was about to join, was one of the survivors of the early efforts to use the new steam power. She had been a full-rigged three-decker with a screw propeller and, in her heyday, had taken part in the Crimean War. Since then ships of many sorts, shapes and sizes had been launched. Shortly before Fisher joined the Navy, the Channel Fleet consisted of ships that were heavily-masted and would neither steam nor sail.

The Navy of 1888 still consisted mainly of ships built to steam or sail, many of a tonnage suitable for police work on foreign stations, but ships without sails and of well-balanced design were now the main strength of the principal Fleet, and it was becoming obvious that the " Groping Age " was drawing to a close and sails would, sooner or later, disappear. But in 1888, and for many years after, an officer who had no experience of sail was regarded as a curiosity, lacking in knowledge and experience of vital importance and certainly no seaman. It was for this reason that the training squadron of corvettes was kept in commission for several years after sail had disappeared from the main fleets, and as late as 1932 a First Lord publicly expressed a wish to revive training in sail on the grounds that it produced qualities that could not be produced in steamships.

In 1888 the Navy was also approaching the end of an " Eccentric Age " for the officers. Though the Fleet had often been engaged in conjoint operations with the Army and in certain wars, such as the Crimean War and Egyptian War, had brought all its resources to bear in support of the Army, it had not been tested in a major maritime war since the fall of Napoleon. For many officers service in the Navy in the later part of the nineteenth century had meant a succession of commissions on foreign stations, often in small ships which spent many months up tropical rivers, and had no electric light, fans, or refrigerators. This form of service tended to exaggerate any slight eccentricities of character and to dull imagination. So in 1888 there were some strange individuals holding senior rank in the Navy. There was a sprinkling of bullies, who made life miserable for all who had the misfortune to serve with them and whose names were a byword in the service. There were captains whose imaginative faculties were so blunted that when examining midshipmen in seamanship they never gave a First Class, even if the candidate answered every question, on the grounds that no midshipman could be a first-class seaman. This gross injustice not infrequently embittered a very promising and keen young officer. There were many senior officers who took no interest whatsoever in the midshipman. They were the " damned young warts " whose slightest fault must be severely punished, yet who, paradoxically, were expected to take complete charge of a large body of seamen on shore or in a boat.

All this was reflected in the entrance examination for the Navy and in the administration and training in the *Britannia*. The examination papers were set by Civil Service Commissioners whose object was apparently to ensure that the crammers lived in affluence. It was extremely difficult for a boy from a preparatory school to take a high place, as some of the subjects of examination were only taught on the classical side and some only on the modern side, and so parents often denied themselves the good things of life in order to pay the higher fees of a crammer. The Navy was beginning to feel the impact of the new discoveries of scientists, metallurgists, and electrical engineers ; but it had not yet occurred to the authorities to attune the training of the future officers of the Fleet to the new conditions. Fortunately for the Navy, the crammers did not monopolise all the vacancies and a few boys, educated at good schools, squeezed in each time. William Fisher was one of these. Though regarded as a certainty for a Winchester Scholarship, he had few marks to spare in this strange examination.

His exceptional knowledge of Greek and History was of no use to him, but Latin and French carried good marks and he found these papers easy. A term mate described him as a highly-strung, shy boy of tall and slight build with very light-coloured hair, and adds that it would have been strange if anyone had picked him from among his fifty-five term mates as the one who would overtop them all and become the outstanding personality of his time. But his term officer, Lieutenant de Robeck, must have seen something the other boys missed, because he was made a cadet captain with prefectorial powers — powers which, when it was a matter of punishment, he exercised with far less satisfaction than that enjoyed by his brother cadet captains.

He had not been a keen games player when he first went to school but by the time he left Lynam's he was a keen Rugby player and in the *Britannia* he began to show aptitude for cricket and won his First XI colours. He never lost his love of that game.

Most of the subjects taught in the *Britannia* in those days were entirely new to the first-term cadets. Seamanship and Navigation filled a large part of the programme ; a feeble attempt was made to teach the cadets some Naval History ; French, Drawing, " Steam " were minor subjects.

The Seamanship instruction was almost entirely confined to " Masts and Yards ". The cadets learned to splice and make the various knots and the details of standing- and running-rigging, and were taken for short cruises in a square-rigged tender. There were " blue boats " for rowing on the Dart and some small cutters, which the senior cadets were allowed to sail on half-holidays.

But a symptom of the age was that the cadets learned nothing about routine and life in a modern man-of-war and it was not unknown for a cadet on watch for the first time in a sea-going ship to report to the officer of the watch " BW for X fall in " without the slightest idea that the mystic letters stood for " both watches for exercise ". Another symptom was the lack of personal touch between the officers and the cadets. The captain and commander were god-like creatures of whom the cadets occasionally caught a glimpse at Divisions or on the playing-fields.

The term-lieutenants were usually appointed for their proficiency at games and often only took a mild interest in their young charges, with the result that the cadets looked for guidance to the term-petty officers, who, though carefully selected, were not always paragons. Fisher's term was fortunate in their officer, as De Robeck not only took an interest in them but was an inspiration to them with his fine physique, proficiency at all games, and perfect manners.

Young Fisher started his naval career in a fair field of competition ; his term mates no longer profited from their cramming and some were feeling the after-effects of being over-crammed, so that he soon began to gain places in the term list.

Cadets who achieved a high percentage in all subjects in the passing-out examination were promoted to midshipmen at once and the others remained naval cadets for several months longer according to their marks.

Fisher set his heart on passing out as a midshipman and worked very hard to that end. His highly-strung temperament gave him some bad hours. To his father he wrote :

The examination in Seamanship begins tomorrow, which I positively dread. I hope you are all quite prepared to see me kicked out at the end of this term.

It was a bitter blow when a few days later his hopes were shattered by his naval instructor :—

My Instructor told me yesterday that I was not to hope for a first class in " study " as he had been watching my papers throughout the whole examination, so I shall have to be contented with eight months, which means that I shall have to wait four months before I am a midshipman. You can imagine how disappointed I am, and I am afraid you will be very disgusted, too. The only consolation is that I think I shall pass high, in the first ten I hope. The French Prize I am sure will not be £20 so no particular interest attaches itself to that. My Instructor told me yesterday that if anyone deserved to pass out a midshipman it was I, but it was very unlucky for me that the Euclid and Trigonometry papers were so hard.

To this letter he added a mournful postscript : " Results will be read out at 12.30 on Sunday morning next but now they are of no interest to me ".

Though when faced with a cruel disappointment, Fisher discounted the importance of the French Prize, it must have been some salve to his wounded pride when he learned that he had won it.

The influence of his home life can be seen in the letters he wrote as a naval cadet. His style and use of language were much in advance of his age and his selection as sub-editor of *The Britannia* showed that his literary gifts had not escaped attention in his new surroundings.

Unlike most boys of his age he was very particular about money matters, and felt a strong aversion to asking his parents for anything beyond his small allowance. He wrote to his father :

Now I have something very disagreeable to say and I hope you will not think me very extravagant, Could you send me some money as I shall want rather a lot in the way of tips ? I am afraid my servant will expect something rather fat and there is a heavy subscription for a present to our instructor.

Do not think I have squandered away all you gave me or run into debt with other fellows, for I have done neither. I am so sorry to end this letter in such a horrid way but I am afraid I shall want about 12/-.

Twelve shillings seems rather an anti-climax after so carefully preparing his father for some shattering demand, but in those days twelve shillings was a large sum for a cadet. In the more enlightened days to come, giving presents to instructors was not countenanced by the officers.

Fisher passed out in July, 1890, and ordered "my chest to be sent to Gieves and my name to be inscribed on the books of the *Duke of Wellington* flagship at Portsmouth, from which I will receive my sailing orders".

NAVAL CADET

JUNIOR STAFF OFFICER, WHALE ISLAND

CHAPTER II

1890-1893

Midshipman, H.M.S. *Raleigh* — Cape Station

FISHER's first sailing-orders told him to join H.M.S. *Raleigh*, flagship of the Cape of Good Hope and West Africa Squadron, shortly returning to her station.

It will be appreciated from the remarks in the foregoing chapter that there were good ships and bad ships for the midshipmen, particularly for the juniors, who having lorded it over the younger cadets during their last term in the *Britannia*, had again to become inferior beings. The sub-lieutenants and senior midshipmen often made life grim for the junior midshipmen, and in many ships the commander and the lieutenants had no idea of what was going on in the gun-room. But service in flagships, particularly on foreign stations, was sought after by officers of all ranks and branches and, as the Admiralty was usually ready to fall in with the wishes of the Commander-in-Chief, he was able to pick his officers and get together a first-rate team. The midshipmen profited, because not only did they learn their job in the best school, but the officers took a personal interest in their games and sports and fostered talent. No doubt young Fisher's father made inquiries when the time came for his son to embark on the big adventure of joining a gun-room and expressed some wishes on the subject to someone in authority. The highly-strung, shy boy who joined the *Britannia* was growing rapidly and gaining strength and confidence, but a good ship on a healthy station would make all the difference during the important three years ahead.

The *Raleigh* was an old ship of 5200 tons displacement, barque-rigged and dependent on sail-power for long passages. She had a curious and mixed armament of muzzle-loading and breech-loading guns and had achieved a speed of 15 knots in her early days. She was typical of the last years of the "Groping Era" and so Fisher's early sea training took place in a ship with main features of two different ages of ship and armament design.

He was told off to be a midshipman of the main cross-trees and to take charge at Action Stations of a 90-cwt M.L. gun and so found himself at once in a position of responsibility.

His first boat was the "blood" boat, so called because it was the boat that brought off the carcases of beef, vegetables and bread from the shore every morning. The term died out with the advent of refrigerators and ships' bakeries. He found the work hard:

> I am very comfortable here only there is such a tremendous lot to do. I really think this is one of the few drawbacks in a naval existence. There is no peace. Not a moment's during the day. Always practising, always exercising. Something continually on the mind. For instance by Friday I have to write up something like 1200 names with ranks and all particulars for the Commander. By tomorrow night I have to show up an account of laying out a stream anchor which, by-the-bye, was exercised this afternoon, occupying four hours and preventing us going ashore tomorrow. My log and a chart have to be ready to go to the Captain on Thursday forenoon. From this you must not think that I am of a discontented frame of mind, but I wish to give you a true account of just what I feel. We get plenty of sleep but now we have begun gymnastic exercises at 6.30 every morning which necessitates getting up at 5.45. This is a mere bagatelle and very good for one.

In after years Fisher used to say that the nearest

approach to hardship he had ever experienced in the Navy was when he was midshipman of the "blood" boat.

The flagship lay a mile or more from the landing-place at Simonstown in a rather exposed anchorage and it often blows hard there. Every morning Fisher turned out with the hands at 4.30 or earlier and by 4.45 was away in charge of his boat. It would still be dark and more often than not a sea running, which would make a wet passage. Then, after embarking his cargo, there would be another rough passage back to the ship to be followed immediately by drill with the other midshipmen if he was in time.

But, though hard work was demanded from both officers and men, the leadership was of a high order and good leadership always evoked Fisher's admiration. He waited some months before mentioning the officers in his letters home and then wrote :

I am going to pass a few remarks upon the officers here and I think I have been here long enough to do so. The lieutenants are nice, in fact very nice without exception. Commander O'Callaghan is one of the best Commanders, it is generally acknowledged, in the service. Not for his smartness or ability but by leniency and well placed kindness with the men. He is certainly a most perfect gentleman. Captain Barrow is nice beyond doubt when off duty, but on duty, I think, as he is quite a newly made Captain, he tries to swagger too much and is rather harsh. Perhaps the fact of his being such a dandy sets me against him rather. You should see him go on inspection rounds in the morning with his beautiful white gloves and cane with uniform. David Nevin, our instructor, is a good old boy who has already taught me a considerable amount and likely to take an interest in me as I have pleased him so far.

But the naval instructor was a broken reed when French was the subject for the day and, as Fisher was keen to improve his French, this annoyed him :—

Old Nevin yesterday took us in French or rather we took him. He was ridiculously ignorant and he defended his bad pronunciation by saying that being an Irishman and having been 20 years at sea, he could hardly expect to know it.

His keen sense of right and wrong was offended when he discovered that the instructor was paid a fee for each French lesson and he longed to expose the fraud. Any injustice, anything not absolutely straight, always roused his indignation. In one letter he expressed himself very strongly about the chaplain, who had informed the men at Divine Service that he would report any man who failed to bring a prayer-book and hymn-book to the service.

But he was very fortunate in his first ship. Midshipmen were at a critical age and there were few ships in which a midshipman would have limited his criticisms of his officers to the naval instructor's shortcomings when teaching French and the chaplain's unchristian behaviour.

Though kept hard at work, the officers kept the old adage in mind and cricket matches and tennis were played whenever and wherever possible. There was usually a cricket ground at the ports visited during the cruises and for the residents the occasional matches against the flagship were the most important features in their fixture list. Fisher's cricket had come on a lot in the *Britannia* and he was soon a member of the *Raleigh*'s XI. At Bathurst, in Gambia, he distinguished himself by making a century against the colony's First XI. He always kept very fit and, if there was no cricket or tennis, obtained his exercise by walking or climbing. He also became keen on billiards, which was one of the attractions of the Naval Club at Simonstown and was often at the rink, where he worked hard to improve his skating.

The programmes of cruises for the ships of the squadron always followed the same general lines — a cruise up the West Coast of Africa, calling at Fernando Po, Sierra

Leone, Bathurst, St. Helena, Ascension, a long stay at Simonstown, and then a cruise up the East Coast calling at Port Elizabeth, Durban, Delagoa Bay, Mombasa, and Zanzibar.

It was fortunate for Fisher that whilst he was in the *Raleigh* the East Coast of Africa as far north as Mombasa was transferred from the East Indies Station to the Cape Station, and so he was able to enlarge his experience of interesting foreign ports and peoples.

It was a grand life for the midshipman. At every port the ship visited they were at once thrown into the swirl of social events, made many new friends, went on shooting expeditions, and played tennis and cricket.

Fisher sometimes found the long periods at Simonstown rather monotonous, but, when he was promoted to a steam-boat, the monotony was relieved by long days away in his boat towing targets for gunnery practice; and there were always the weekly field days when the small-arm companies and field guns were landed for mimic warfare, which he greatly enjoyed and which gave him a chance of exercising command and using his powerful voice. His family had friends at the Cape, and amongst others Lady Loch often asked him to Government House. He described her as "a pleasant-looking lady of majestic proportions". She became a lifelong friend and was the last person he went to see before leaving England to take up his appointment as Commander-in-Chief, Mediterranean. One of his week-ends at Government House was cut short by being re-called to his ship, as the midshipman who had lent him a pair of trousers wanted them himself!

Fisher was serving in the *Raleigh* at a period of our history when small wars, in which the Navy and the Army operated together, were quite frequent, and he and his messmates were always hoping that trouble would blow up somewhere on the station. On one occasion their hopes were raised by a signal from the Commander-in-Chief ordering all ships to complete with fuel and prepare for sea as there was some trouble brewing with the Portuguese at Lorenço Marques. He wrote, " we have all been too excited to speak almost ". But they were doomed to disappointment, as only one ship, not the flagship, was eventually sent.

Another disappointment, of a much less serious nature, was when some Zulu chiefs came on board. Fisher and his messmates expected to see " enormous burly men with rings and tattoos and no vestige of clothing, but instead, two old men, one in a very seedy black coat and striped breeches, all frayed at the ends, and the other not much smarter " came on board. They were terribly frightened and made curious gestures when some guns were fired for their edification. Boys are often disillusioned when they see the great ones of the earth in the flesh.

In those days midshipmen often served the last few months of their time in the Training Squadron of sailing corvettes and Fisher and five others received orders to return home and join the *Calypso* after they had been nearly three years on the Africa Station.

Though he must have been sorry to say good-bye to a ship in which he had spent three happy years and to officers for whom he had unbounded admiration and affection, the prospect of seeing his parents and brothers and sisters again must have been thrilling to a young man whose devotion to his family was so strong. It is apposite to quote a passage from one of his letters to his mother when he was only seventeen :

> I hate hearing of everyone being so ill and the work devolving on you. For goodness' sake (I would use a stronger term if it were polite) keep well and don't wear yourself to death. Take it easy. Why cannot you gratify my wish for a short time.

So after three years on the Cape Station the frail little classical scholar returned a robust son of Anak with a passion for his profession, which showed the wisdom of his boyish choice.

The best description of his life on the Cape Station is in an article, " The Midshipman's Return ", which he wrote for the *English Review* thirty-three years later :

THE MIDSHIPMAN'S RETURN

To go away for three years when you are only fifteen is to say good-bye to home for ever — and at the end of that time to get orders by telegraph to return to England " by next Government opportunity " seems little short of a miracle — the recall of an outcast to a life that is almost forgotten, the thread of which has been lost.

It was over thirty years ago that I and five others were ordered home from the fine frigate in which we had travelled many thousands of miles, under sail and steam. We were excited at the thought of change. We enjoyed our farewell dinner in the gun-room, our last night in our hammocks and the thought of no more night watches for a bit, no more sail-drill — but for me it was not till we got much nearer England that thoughts of home took definite shape. An awkward corner had to be rounded before I actually got away. There was my old Malay washerman to pay, my club bill, a tailor — the first account had been a monthly anxiety ever since I had been on the station. It used not to be more than fifteen shillings, the club bill about half that, and to the tailor I owed a guinea. Now, a midshipman who could not meet his washing bill was looked upon almost as a felon. " Jones hasn't paid his washing bill this month ! " Could anything more awful be said of him in the gun-room, and how could such a crime fail to reach the commander's ears ? The old Malay himself might report it. Assets half a sovereign. Really this " going home " was no joke. Time was short. No midshipman that I had ever heard of had left the station " owing money all over the place ". What a name to leave behind one ! Make a clean breast of it to one of the lieutenants and borrow with a promise to pay as soon as one got home ? In those days a midshipman was one thing and a lieutenant very much another. Anyhow, I decided it was utterly out of the question ; and then suddenly came relief, though disguised as the final crushing blow. A large parcel lay on the gun-room table — a customs officer inquiring for me — 9s. 6d. duty to pay on the contents, which turned out to be a new blue serge suit, two pairs of flannel trousers, flannel shirts, brown boots, with odds and ends of collars and ties. The cargo I had been so long waiting for from home, and which I had asked should be sent to meet me at Zanzibar, had turned up at Simonstown just in time, but somewhat en-cumbered. The duty was paid ; I was practically penniless ; but if and when I got home, at least I should be decently dressed.

My old plain clothes, old flannels, and shirts were put up to auction, and the proceeds satisfied the club and the wash-ing. The tailor — a nasty, nagging man — became more and more importunate. We were to sail tomorrow from Cape Town in one of the old Indian troopers. In great dejection I went ashore for a last walk along the dusty, windswept coast road, and stopped to talk to the cobbler who had been in the habit of patching up my boots for so long. He was almost blind, and being toothless was difficult to understand. I told him he would no longer be set such difficult tasks by me, for I was homeward bound. The dear old fellow looked at me as if he was almost sorry, and because of it I unburdened myself to him. Without a word he slowly hoisted himself up, hobbled into his shop and returned with a sovereign. He made no mention of paying back, but I didn't forget him when I got home. The slight matter of the railway fare to Cape Town was adjusted by my being put officially in charge of a draft of time-expired seamen, and thus I got a Govern-ment pass and joined the troopship a clear threepenny-bit to the good.

We midshipmen were berthed on the lower deck aft in what was called the Pandemonium, with bunks, not ham-mocks, to sleep in, and we thought this palatial. The ship was full of military details, many of the officers' wives and families being on board as well.

It was a most delightful voyage home — we had only the

smallest duties given to us, and the novelty of being in a steamship that could actually hold her course and keep steadily punching every second nearer England whatever the wind and weather was incredible.

How jolly to think of all that had happened since the day when outward bound I was straining my eyes for the first sight of Table Mountain — a small boy of fifteen !

I had sailed a good many thousands of miles since then ; St. Helena — well known from three or four visits — was connected chiefly in my mind with the charming French family officially entrusted with the care of Napoleon's tomb. Some of us midshipmen used to steal ashore — with or without leave — after dinner at night and do that very arduous walk up the rugged path to Longwood, and dance in the old barn, or play hockey on the green if there was a moon. There were enough daughters to go round, and all pretty, and those nights, notwithstanding sprained ankles coming home down the hill, stand out as specially happy ones.

Sun-scorched Ascension, with its turtles and strange sea-birds, we knew also, and Sierra Leone was very familiar. There was little for midshipmen to do ashore there. I used to walk out and bathe in the Judges' Pool — a small pond about two miles from Freetown — the path there was a pretty one through a forest, and I liked to watch the monkeys swinging overhead. I remember one afternoon meeting about a dozen black boys of about my own age and, whilst I was dressing, watching the water dry out in patches on their oily skins. They came from a school with English masters and spoke English perfectly. Before many minutes our conversation became a sort of educational duel. Arithmetic, algebra, Latin, we fired back at one another, Greek even, and I was hard put to it to hold my own.

Bathurst I should like to see again, and Accra, where one lands through the surf. The latter is associated in my mind with a great cricket match and a dignity ball at which the black girls appeared in low-necked dresses and insisted on the greatest punctilio of deportment. " No etiquette," they would say, if asked to dance without an introduction, at the same time indicating some unsavoury-looking gentleman in a bright red tie who would carry out the necessary formalities.

Fernando Po with its dense jungle, huge butterflies, and primitive forest men (pigmies) we knew — we had had a taste of tornadoes, too, and in a sailing ship they are unforgettable. St. Paul de Loanda, Walfisch Bay, Saldanha Bay, where we shot buck, and far-off Tristan d'Acunha we have visited — I was glad to have been to Tristan d'Acunha, a wonderful conical mountain rising straight out of the sea, visible at a great distance. We brought the colony their yearly mail, also the Bishop of St. Helena to baptize, confirm, and marry. But, as usual in those stormy latitudes, the bishop could not land, and the islanders had to walk round to the lee side and come on board us. They were an unhealthy, inbred collection of people, with shoes made of rough hide or sea-bird skins, and tattered apparel, but part owners of great herds of oxen, sheep, and goats. In exchange for beef we gave them candles, cocoa, oatmeal, rifles, and ammunition; their herds had become so wild that a rifle was necessary.

We took back some twenty of these descendants of Old Peter Green to the Cape, but I fear that the transplanting was little to their good, and they did not long survive.

It was real sailorising in those latitudes — the "roaring forties". Many a time did the whole middle watch pass reefing topsails. I used to enjoy the weather yard-arm more than the lee. It took a long time to "light out to windward" and to "pass the weather ear-ring", but it was more comfortable to be that side than dangling from the yard-arm overhanging and dipping close to the crested seas.

The east coast we had got to know well, too. We had lain for weeks in Delagoa Bay in the greatest state of excitement anticipating orders to land and take the Portuguese town of Ponta Delgada. Mozambique was more familiar to me than Dartmouth, and Zanzibar, where I met Tippoo Tib and Sir H. H. Johnston, was frequently visited. At sunset I used generally to find myself in the square of the Sultan's palace to hear his army band play the Zanzibar Anthem, which sounded very fine. The tune is as fresh in my memory as is the odd sickly smell of native life and sandalwood which permeated the narrow streets.

In those days there were slave dhows and boat cruising from ships of the squadron and occasional skirmishes, and a little farther north at Mombasa, or south at the Pungwee River, there was big game to be shot.

And now I was on my way home to tell my father and mother, my brothers and sisters, of all that I had seen and done.

I did not grudge a single day of that three weeks' voyage home. The dinners in the big saloon were great fun, and, as we got nearer home and got to know everyone better, the fun increased. One fiery little major showed how to crack a walnut on the table with his forehead. Of course, " for the honour of the service ", we had to follow suit. Soon every officer felt similarly bound, and thus it came about that after the port had circulated a regular *feu de joie* passed up and down the long table, and handkerchiefs were seen mopping the blood from many a brow ; the trick, of course, is that if the head is brought down with sufficient force, it is the nut that cracks and not the head. It is the timorous who suffer scars, and many stepped ashore in England severely marked.

We anchored at Spithead on a most beautiful August morning, and as hot a day as any that we had had on the voyage home across the equator. The excitement of getting ashore ! But before going to the station a few formalities of reporting our arrival to the naval authorities had to be gone through, and a letter to be got from my outfitters with money. I learnt that all was well at home, my home in Surrey between Guildford and Dorking. And now what train could I catch ? It is early afternoon. If I hurry I can just catch one that will get me home about four. I decide against that — I must send a telegram first — there must be no surprise. I want a properly staged welcome. I shall start at about five — it is a slow train, and I don't reach home by it till after seven — but it is the train for me.

And so, telegram sent, I turn into the public gardens, near the Portsmouth town station, and in warm sunshine sit and wait. There is the town hall clock to keep me straight, there are lovely flower-beds to look at, such as I had not seen for three years, and the *va-et-vient* of such a spot is not uninteresting. And I shall get home at the end of the day, just as I had always planned. I don't quite know why, but a home-coming has always seemed to me to be an affair of the evening. It is incongruous at 11 A.M. or 2 P.M., but just perfect at 7 P.M.

I have walked through the gardens hundreds of times since and seen masts and yards, then visible over the chimney-pots of old Portsmouth, give place to the fighting-tops of the modern battleship ; but I have never forgotten that afternoon of glowing anticipation.

I stir myself at last and make for the station. I feel an almost irresistible impulse to tell every guard, inspector, and porter that I am home today from foreign lands, and I believe I do tell a good many. The train loiters — never mind, I have scarcely been in any sort of train for years. It is a glorious evening. The scent of new-mown grass, flowers, bracken, woods, and farms, which makes so strong an impression on a sailor long unfamiliar with such things, can be enjoyed at leisure. The country folk who get in and out are steeped in the scent of the country. At Guildford I change ; ten minutes' pacing the platform, and I am off along the branch line. It is the last of the evening. I am now keenly on the watch for every well-known landmark, at the bend of the line I have head and shoulders out of the window, and as I see the loom of the country station I feel the brakes. Yes, there is a little group there. I wave my hat, and the next second five brothers followed by my father are running alongside my door. They look very tall, and are all in flannels, four older than me, and one younger.

The family cricket match against the village just over. Inconsequent questions and answers. My mother and sisters waiting at home so as not to be too over-whelming at the station. Luggage brings one to earth again. It is put in the carriage, and I drive slowly away with my father, the others hanging on behind. Half-way up the hill I see figures in white in the dusk, and the next moment I am out of the carriage and surrounded by sisters. Sisters let themselves go in a way that brothers don't, and I shall never forget those soft, yet excited, voices, nor the sudden realisation of what I had been banished from so long.

When I reach my mother, I am the centre of a crowd, each one pointing out in what respect I have changed, whilst I am trying to fit myself into my old niche in the family. Unconsciously and, I hope, humbly I measure myself against my brothers. How quick they are with their jokes and allusions! By comparison I see myself slow, stupid, a bit pompous and tongue-tied, but what matters? I am home again — no longer alone.

CHAPTER III

1893 - 1898

Midshipman, H.M.S. *Calypso*, Training Squadron — Acting Sub-Lieutenant's Courses — Sub-Lieutenant and Lieutenant, H.M.S. *Hawke*, Mediterranean Fleet

THE Training Squadron, which consisted of four barque-rigged corvettes, was the Navy's counterpart of a crammer's establishment for public school boys who wished to be brought up to the necessary standard for entering a University or the Army. Midshipmen were sent to the Squadron to be "topped up" for the seamanship examination for sub-lieutenant and batches of young seamen were drafted to the ships before each cruise. The captains and officers were all good seamen, specially picked for their experience in "sail". Though it was obvious that the days of sail were numbered, it was still considered to be the only school at which officers could acquire a seaman's eyes, alertness, and power of quick decision in emergency.

The Training Squadron survived long after Fisher's day and many officers expressed gloomy forebodings when training in sail was finally abandoned. That happened when every penny of the naval estimates was urgently required to build up a fleet of the new type powerful battleships, cruisers, and destroyers, but was also inevitable when officers and petty officers thoroughly versed in the ways of a sailing ship were no longer available. It was a trade that could only be learned by experience and disaster would have soon followed any attempt to man a sailing ship with a personnel who did not know their work thoroughly.

Life for Fisher in the *Calypso* was very different from the pleasant, though often busy, life of the Cape Station. No more cricket, skating, billiards, and visiting interesting places. Officers and men were kept hard at work with constant sail drill. It was a very welcome life to him, as he had set his heart on obtaining a First Class in seamanship, and he thoroughly enjoyed the occasional opportunities of standing on the poop and using his powerful voice to roar down the topgallant and royal yards or " make all plain sail ".

On the fateful day, 7th July, 1894, he was fortunate in appearing before a board of officers who had no ridiculous obsessions that a midshipman could never know enough to be given a First Class and he came through with flying colours.

His captain wrote on his certificate " He is a good leader of men ", which was high praise in a world where so much store was laid on ability to command and where the standard was very high.

With the passing of the examination Fisher became an acting sub-lieutenant. He was now nineteen and a half, and for the next few months had to bend his mind and energies to passing four other examinations, in theoretical subjects, gunnery, pilotage, and torpedo. Acting sub-lieutenants were sent for a short period to shore establishments to be crammed for the examinations, though they were supposed to have learnt all that was necessary during their three years at sea. Some of the young officers, who had served in ships where no one had troubled about their education, had considerable difficulty in squeezing through, but Fisher had been fortunate in his first ship and was hoping to obtain First Class certificates in all the examinations and thus gain early promotion to lieutenant.

Theoretical subjects were taken first and for those

the young officers were sent to the Royal Naval College, Greenwich. The first day at the College was an exciting one, as the *Britannia* cadets, who had said good-bye to one another nearly four years before, met again for the first time.

A class-mate gives an interesting glimpse of Fisher at this period :

Whatever his term mates at Dartmouth had thought of him, now, when they met again after four years' dispersal over the seven seas, they had to recognise a tall, well set-up fellow, assured in manner, good-humoured, able to hold his own in all ways and more often than not to take a leading part in what was going forward.

He was already emerging as the leading spirit of his time, and his exuberant spirits must have sometimes led him into a clash with authority as his certificate from the captain contained the significant words " as a rule satisfactory ".

It must have been a severe blow to a young man of Fisher's temperament when the results were announced and he learned that he had just failed to obtain a First Class. He had got on well with his instructor in the *Raleigh*, but in his letters home he complained of the stuffiness of the cabin which was used as a schoolroom, and admitted that, having been up and doing as a rule since 4.30 A.M., he found it infernally difficult to keep awake.

The short cramming period at the College was not sufficient to bring his knowledge up to the high standard required for a First Class, but at the Gunnery School at Whale Island, where he went next, he came into his own. Whale Island was still in what was humorously called the " Gas and Gaiters " era. The school bore a high reputation for smartening up officers and men. Parade drills comprised a large part of all the courses of instruction and a principal qualification for a staff officer or petty officer was that he should be a "smart drill". The great parade echoed to the roar of orders given in stentorian tones to squads, companies, and battalions, and a high spot was the weekly field-gun battery drill, when eight field-guns, drawn by crews of sixteen men, were manœuvred and unlimbered, and created so much noise and dust in the process that only an officer with a very penetrating voice could control their movements. The gunnery renaissance had not yet begun and the instruction at big and small guns was mainly confined to drill and "stripping", a term used for learning the names and purposes of all the mechanisms and dismembering and reassembling them. There were as yet no "dotters", "deflection teachers", and "loaders" for training gunlayers, trainers, sightsetters, and loading numbers. Fisher revelled in this scene of bustle and smartness in which there were so many opportunities of exercising command and he obtained his First Class without difficulty. In pilotage he also obtained a First Class but, strangely, he suffered a second disappointment over his examination in torpedo. This is difficult to explain, as the torpedo examination was not regarded as so difficult a fence as the others. There was no chance of exercising command in the *Vernon*, and the atmosphere of the establishment would not have appealed to him, for in those days the *Vernon*'s boast was that it was the exact opposite of its rival, Whale Island, in its mode of life. No parades, no attempts at smartness, officers and men usually in sweaters and sea boots. The officers claimed they were the seamen of the Navy and all that Whale Island did was "to play at soldiers". Sea boots and sweaters were the right rig for handling torpedoes, fitting out boats for mine-laying, and going afloat in all weathers in torpedo-boats and launches, but it is not without interest to record that when the old three-deckers that formed the *Vernon* of those days were no longer suitable and the torpedo school was housed on shore in the Gun Wharf at Portsmouth, the *Vernon* began to vie with the other naval establishments in the smartness of her parades and men, and at the same time dealt with far more complicated torpedoes, mines, and electrical equipment than formerly.

Fisher attributed his failure in the *Vernon* to not replacing the little screw in the oil-bottle of a torpedo he had put together from mixed-up component parts but, though some of the examining officers no doubt had strange notions about marking, the truth probably was that he had learned very little about *Vernon* subjects in the *Raleigh* and *Calypso* and could not make up enough leeway in a few weeks. That certainly was the experience of many sub-lieutenants of that day. Three firsts and two seconds was, however, considered a very creditable result and carried accelerated promotion to lieutenant.

Though for those four months Fisher worked like a demon, he was able to snatch happy days with his family. There were a few days' leave between courses and short week-end leave during the courses. London was within reach of Greenwich, and, though the train service was not up to modern standards, there was always a hansom cab for those who missed the last train. Fisher made full use of those opportunities of re-establishing the close bonds which had knit together the brothers and sisters before the four-years separation.

In January, 1896 he was appointed sub-lieutenant of the *Hawke*, one of the smartest ships in the smart Mediterranean Fleet. All the energy and imagination that had gone to produce extreme smartness in the sailing-era had now been focussed on producing similar smartness in the all-steam fleet. Instead of striving to reduce by one more second the time to cross top-gallant and royal yards or shift topsail yards, the effort was to reduce by a fraction of a second the time for "out net defence". The anchors, too, offered splendid opportunities for competitive drills and the best times for placing the heavy bower-anchor under the ship's launch or laying out a stream-anchor were as well known to the officers and men of the Fleet as the best times for the hundred yards or mile were known to track athletes. The Monday morning drills were the subject of keen speculation and meticulous preparation throughout the Fleet on Sunday evening. A smart yeoman of signals, watching every move on the flagship's signal deck, would take a chance and rap out the purport of the signal when the first flag showed above the netting and, though this sometimes led to disaster, the saving of that second might enable his ship to " break the one pendant ", the signal for evolution completed, first, and to be first at drills was the main object of every officer and man. It was some years before this was replaced by a very different object — to be first at the annual gunlayers' test ; and some years later that the object became to be the best ship at long-range battle practice. The other object, and one which has fortunately never changed throughout the ages, was to be the cleanest and most highly-decorated and polished ship in the Fleet. Commanders vied with one another to produce the whitest deck and often stinted themselves and cut down their recreation and amusements to pay for polishing materials, wooden gratings and brass fittings.

As the commanders' and first lieutenants' promotions depended on the performance of their ship at drills and her smartness, acute centralisation was the custom of the day. The commander was up with the hands every morning to see the decks scrubbed and was always prowling round the decks in working hours. He left as little as possible to the junior officers. Succeeding generations of naval officers often expressed surprise at this absorption in evolutions and cleanliness to the exclusion of interest in the armament, which was the reason for the existence of the ship; but the battle-efficiency of the armament in any period can only be judged in relation to that of other navies. The Kaiser had not yet set his heart on building a navy to challenge us and the French Fleet, the only possible opponent, was at the same stage of armament development; if war had broken out, battles would have been fought unscientifically at short range with each big gun or battery of small guns controlled independently by the officer in charge, and superior smartness at drill and a superior fighting spirit would have been the deciding factors.

Despite the high degree of centralisation, the junior officers came into their own at the drills, when each had a responsible job and there were also small evolutions two or three evenings a week conducted by the officer of the watch. Fisher must have been delighted to find himself in a ship whose name was a byword for smartness.

Long after the *Hawke* had left the main Fleet for the reserve, she was remembered as the ship whose stream anchor was kept burnished like polished silver; that was going one better than any of her competitors.

Even in that numerous company of officers who placed such high value on "command" and ability to get the very best out of the ship's companies, Fisher was outstanding and it was said of him in Malta: "If you want to know how boats should be hoisted, listen to and watch the *Hawke* when Fisher is the officer of the watch. You can hear him all over the Grand Harbour, and the men run the boats up at a furious pace." Both his captains, W. de V. Hamilton and Sir Richard Poore, were much struck with his character and ability and sent highly appreciative reports to the Admiralty.

Thanks to the classes he obtained in his examinations, he only had to wait six months for promotion to lieutenant and, after a year's service in that rank, he had to make up his mind if he was to become a specialist officer or remain a " salt-horse " lieutenant.

Today, the majority of lieutenants specialise in gunnery, torpedo, signals, navigation, submarines, anti-submarine work, or as pilots and observers of the Fleet Air Arm, but in Fisher's day the only specialists were gunnery, torpedo, and navigation officers, and, as promotion for the latter was not then good, there was no keen competition for the Navigation Course.

Fisher's aptitude for command and his success in his first gunnery examination naturally led his thoughts towards gunnery and, when he made his decision, his captain had no hesitation in backing his request strongly. He was a young man who thought deeply about his profession and, though he felt the call of the parade, he also realised that gunnery would sooner or later offer a rich field of endeavour and something beyond stripping and gun drill for him to sharpen his wits on.

Competition for the gunnery course ran high but Fisher, whose name was known far outside his ship and immediate circle of friends, was one of the certainties for the course that commenced on 14th September, 1898.

Among the other fortunate applicants were A. A. M. Duff, F. Larken, P. T. H. Beamish, and E. A. Taylor. Both the first two named rose to the rank of Admiral and held important commands ; both the last two named became Members of Parliament after long and distinguished service in the Navy.

Those two years in the *Hawke* left a deep impression on Fisher's mind. The places visited and their inhabitants aroused his keen interest. Well versed in the Classics, he got more enjoyment from his rambles ashore than most of his brother officers ; the scenery, the colour of the sea, the sky and the countryside all stirred his senses and satisfied his love of beautiful things ; and it was at this period that he began to feel an interest in the Maltese people, which in time grew into real affection and which, as will be seen later, manifested itself in many practical forms when he held positions of authority in the Mediterranean Fleet.

CHAPTER IV

1898-1906

Gunnery Lieutenant's Course, Greenwich and Whale Island — Junior Staff Officer, Whale Island — Gunnery Lieutenant, H.M.S. *Canopus*, Mediterranean Fleet — Senior Staff Officer, H.M.S. *Cambridge* — Senior Staff Officer, Whale Island — "*Venerable* Firings" — First and Gunnery Lieutenant, H.M.S. *King Edward VII* — Promoted to Commander

THE courses for officers qualifying as gunnery lieutenants underwent many changes when the great expansion of the Fleet to meet the German challenge began and when, concurrently, the gunnery renaissance initiated by Captain Percy Scott radically altered the form of instruction.

But when Fisher was selected for the September 1898 course the urgent need for a large number of gunnery lieutenants to be qualified as quickly as possible had not appeared, and the qualifiers spent a year at Greenwich, a year at Whale Island, and a year on the staff of one of the schools.

When a sub-lieutenant, Fisher had suffered a disappointment at Greenwich but now he started level with his thirty-one class-mates and easily obtained a First Class in mathematics and physics, the same subjects that he had failed to master in the stuffy cabin of the *Raleigh*.

He soon became the dominant figure amongst that band of specially-selected officers and it was at Greenwich that he was given the title of "The Old Champion", which stuck to him all his life.

Fisher was also responsible for giving humorous

nicknames to his class-mates and his lambent brain was always busy inventing new nicknames for his friends and his family when writing to them.

He was the life and soul of that long course. "Who is going to take on the Old Champion?" he would shout after school hours, and whether it were racquets, tennis, or billiards, it was certain to be a lively game, accompanied by an amusing running commentary on what the "O.C." would or would not do to his opponent. These threats were no doubt often fulfilled but not always, because, though he played every game with tremendous vigour, he never devoted enough time to any one game to become a first-class performer.

The Greenwich course gave him many opportunities of seeing his family and friends. There were the long week-ends and there was also a long summer leave, which, though it interfered with the lieutenants' and sub-lieutenants' courses, was necessary for the instructing staff who were permanent and many of them well advanced in years.

Armed with a First Class in the more difficult theoretical subjects, Fisher approached the next stage in high spirits. Whale Island was still the same as he had known it as a sub-lieutenant and he was returning to the parade and field battery drills at which he knew he shone, with his fine presence and stentorian voice. Amongst the staff officers were F. C. T. Tudor, W. R. Hall, O. de B. Brock, and G. P. W. Hope, all of whom rose to positions of eminence. That Fisher was acquiring a commanding position amongst his contemporaries is clear from the following story told by one of them. "The curriculum included the preparing and giving of a lecture by each student before the Captain and staff of the school and his fellow students — a dreaded ordeal. Fisher was one of the last to lecture. Any nervousness or idiosyncrasies of the previous lecturers had been seized upon by him for subsequent chaff, so the class were on the lookout to retaliate. But he took the wind out of our sails. His subject was the work of the Naval Brigade in the South African War, and compared with the previous efforts of the others it was a *tour de force*. In the interest they took, the class forgot to search for ammunition they had hoped to get to return Fisher's fire of good-humoured ridicule. I think it was now that his class-mates realised that Fisher had powers which enabled him to do many things a good deal better than was possible for them."

The captain of the *Excellent* — the name of the original gunnery training ship was still retained — was W. H. May, and he must have been struck by Fisher's outstanding personality, for he remembered him when, as Commander-in-Chief, Atlantic Fleet, he was looking for a gunnery lieutenant for his flagship the *King Edward VII*.

After a year's hard work and hard play in very congenial surroundings, Fisher passed out high with a First Class certificate and was selected for the Junior Staff at Whale Island. It was the ambition of the qualifiers, unless their homes were near one of the other two gunnery schools at Devonport and Chatham, to stay at Whale Island, as it was the principal and largest school, where all officers were trained in gunnery and where the experimental work was carried out.

As a staff officer, Fisher's powers of command were given full play. It was the staff officers who took command of the large parades and who were responsible for keeping the drill instruction in the gun-batteries at a high standard. There were also lectures to be given to sub-lieutenants and much of a staff officer's time was devoted to examining officers and seamen.

Remembering that fatal torpedo oil-bottle screw that caused him so much disappointment in the *Vernon*, he was, no doubt, an examiner who kept to straightforward questions and did not try to trick the examinees into a mistake — a not uncommon practice at that time.

But, enjoyable as a staff officer's life must have been to him, he must often have been thinking of the next and biggest step in a gunnery lieutenant's career — his first ship. There were still old ships in the Fleet which did not give much scope to the gunnery lieutenant and, as each junior staff officer's time approached for going to sea, he prayed that his luck would be in and that a vacancy would occur in the most modern and largest ship afloat.

Fisher was thrilled when he was told that he was to join the *Canopus* in November, 1901. She was a modern battleship in the Mediterranean Fleet. " My one feeling is now impatience to get to the *Canopus* ; I'll wake them up when I get there ", he wrote.

During the three years since he had left the *Hawke*, life in the Mediterranean Fleet had undergone radical changes. Two powerful forces were exercising a profound influence on the Navy — Sir John Fisher, Commander-in-Chief, and Captain Percy Scott.

Sir John Fisher's career had been a remarkable one. As a young lieutenant he had been recognised as an officer of rare accomplishments and in every subsequent rank he had left his mark on the service. Now, for the first time, he was in command of a large fleet and putting into practice new and sometimes startling ideas on fleet work and training for battle, which he had been nursing and perfecting for years. There is one interesting reference to this astonishing man in Fisher's letters :

> I went to a lecture by Jacky Fisher on Naval Gunnery and Strategy ; he hardly used a single note and talked for two hours, simply magnificent. Very interesting and humorous too. His smile is irresistible.

Officers who could not keep the pace demanded by the Commander-in-Chief got short shrift, but it was a golden age for the young who were efficient and enterprising, as Jacky's eagle eye soon detected merit amongst the junior officers.

Percy Scott had startled the navies of all the maritime Powers when a cruiser he commanded obtained a percentage of hits at the annual gunlayers' test that was beyond the dreams of the most enthusiastic gunnery officers. There had never been anything amiss in the manufacture of the guns and their ammunition and, if aimed correctly, the shot would hit the bull's-eye; but, until Scott bent his brilliant mind to solving the problem, the sighting apparatus was so inadequate that even the best and steadiest gunlayers often failed to obtain any hits. That being so, there was nothing to inspire gunnery lieutenants to invent appliances for the training of the gunlayers and sightsetters or to induce keenness to improve the rate of loading. But, once Scott had produced his telescopic sight, everything else followed, with Scott always in the van of the inventors.

So, though the enthusiasm for evolutions and for smartness in appearance had in no way abated since his *Hawke* days, there was now superimposed new and even more strenuous competition to be first at the gunlayers' test; and this was almost entirely the business of the gunnery officer.

A few years earlier a gunnery lieutenant was fortunate if serving with a commander who would let him have the guns' crews once a week for training and it was not unknown for an after-turret to remain in the locked position all the commission so as not to tarnish the enamel paint by firing the guns; but now a request for some of the guns' crews every day was met without much ado in a ship of the Mediterranean Fleet, because Jacky Fisher was calling the tune and it would be of little avail for a commander to boast of the beauty of his enamelled surfaces and the high polish on the brightwork if the ship made a poor showing at her firings.

Nevertheless Fisher was more fortunate than many gunnery officers who were looked on as rather a nuisance and disturbers of the ordered routine of the ship and who received little assistance in their difficult task from their messmates or their captain, if they were not under the spell of Percy Scott or the eye of Jacky Fisher.

Fisher's delight at the prospect of holding a responsible position in this new world of bustle and well-directed effort, and in a ship with up-to-date officers, was great. He wrote to his father when waiting at Malta for his ship to return from a cruise :

> When I tell you that the *Canopus* has just this very moment come into harbour, a vision of beauty, you will understand my feelings at the present moment. I would not change places this morning with your friend, Albert Edward.

Though he had written, " I'll wake them up when I get there ", he must have looked forward with slight apprehension to his relations with the commander, A. C. Leveson, a redoubtable figure who, as first lieutenant of Whale Island, had established the tautest régime in its history and had caused many a young officer to vow he would never again set foot on the Island. Both officers and men were overawed by this strong and ruthless personality. Fisher, however, was now himself a strong and determined man, not easily overawed by anyone and on joining he remarked to some of his friends in the mess, " I hear this is a one-man ship. I'm going to see that she becomes a two-man ship."

His first meeting with Leveson was a good augury for friendly co-operation. " He shook hands very cordially. He is very good-looking, clean-shaven, broad forehead, and striking eyes." From that moment those two strong characters, who might so easily have clashed, found much to admire in one another and, though it is hard to believe that Leveson ever surrendered his dominating position, it was said in the Fleet that after six months the *Canopus* was still a one-man ship, but that one man was Fisher, still only a lieutenant of six years' standing, with three or four lieutenants senior to him in the ship.

Fisher undoubtedly brought a new and much-wanted note of cheerfulness to the ship. One of his messmates, the chaplain, wrote :

Take my word for it, he was a very live wire on board and kept everyone keen and jolly in the wardroom, always ready for a rag. He had nicknames for all of us which stuck, and we always called him " The Champion ". There were lots of very amusing things he did and organised among us officers. With all his splendid go and high spirits, he had a serious side and we had many a helpful talk on the deeper things, Religion, Philosophy, and life generally.

Fisher, on his side, was extremely happy with his messmates and could always find congenial companions for a game of racquets or tennis, or for the journeys of exploration he so loved to organise when the ship anchored in new surroundings.

Mention can fittingly be made here of Fisher's love of music which he was able to gratify at Malta. At the Opera House he could hear grand opera at a small cost and he never missed an opportunity. In a letter he expresses his fury at a female who, having stated that soldiers and midshipmen bored her terribly, went on to talk through the best parts of *La Traviata*, a special favourite of his. " An opera named *La Bohême* is on next Saturday ", he wrote to a friend. " Beg, borrow, or steal the money to hear it. It's divine. If you haven't the money, I will pay you for your ticket."

All good commissions come to an end. This was just as well because it would have been asking too much of human nature to expect officers and men, who were kept to such a pitch as those of the *Canopus*, to keep up the pace beyond three years. With Leveson as commander and Fisher as gunnery lieutenant, the *Canopus* had acquired a great reputation for smartness and gunnery efficiency in a Fleet in which Sir John Fisher insisted on an exceptionally high standard; but by the spring of 1903 she had been three years in commission and was due to pay off and recommission, and Fisher said good-bye to a ship in which he had greatly enhanced his reputation as a leader of men and as an original thinker, and to messmates for whom he had the greatest affection and who regarded him as the mainspring of all the fun and good things that had brightened their lives.

A gunnery lieutenant who had proved himself during his first term of service was a likely candidate for the senior staff of one of the gunnery schools and Fisher spent seven months at the West Country Gunnery School, H.M.S. *Cambridge*. He was then given the coveted appointment of a senior staff officer at Whale Island, coveted because the first lieutenant was always chosen for one of the youngest promotions to commander.

Percy Scott was now the captain, busy revolutionising the training.

When Fisher was serving in the *Canopus*, the dawn of a new era of gunnery had broken on the Navy. The immense energy, coupled with the imagination of the gunnery lieutenants, that had been directed to improving the performance of the guns at short-range firings at a fixed target, had produced in a very short time an all-round high standard, which a few years earlier would have been considered impossible. It was inevitable that the more progressive-minded senior officers and the younger keen gunnery lieutenants should begin to look beyond this short-range firing by single guns, and should be eager to examine the possibilities of hitting a moving target at long range with equal accuracy and with all guns firing together.

There were many problems to solve. Range-finders would have to be far more accurate at long range and not lose accuracy when shaken by the ship's movement in a seaway; reliable means of communication between a central-control position and the gun positions would have to be designed and fitted; some means of keeping the range of a moving target that was free to alter course and speed would have to be found; and a system of "spotting" orders established by a series of trials.

It was a great opportunity for gunnery officers. Fisher was in the van of the new crusade and his quick grasp of essentials and his fertile imagination played a large part in solving the many new problems that appeared at each stage of development. To be a smart officer and a good "drill" had hitherto been the principal requirements for a senior staff officer; now he had not only to fulfil those requirements, but had to be a recognised leader in the drive for efficient gun performance at the new battle ranges.

Fisher took up his new duties on 1st January, 1909, but was at once sent out to the Mediterranean to watch and report on the "*Venerable* firings". That series of firings altered the course of gunnery history. For several months the *Venerable*, a modern battleship, steamed up and down firing at a target at about 7000 yards, then considered the longest range at which the broadside fire could be effective and efficiently controlled, and by trial and error a system of control was evolved for adoption in the Fleet. Fisher's presence at these trials was most important, as it was essential that the training of the officers and men at the gunnery schools should be attuned to the latest developments afloat. The commander of the *Venerable* was A. E. M. Chatfield, already recognised as a coming man and destined to be the outstanding naval figure of a later age.

Fisher's career now took a most unusual course as he did not remain on the senior staff to become first lieutenant. Before he had completed his first year, he fell out with

Percy Scott. Scott sent for him one day and lectured him for two hours about the new methods of training he wished adopted. Fisher worked long into the night putting down on paper what he thought Scott wanted but, when he presented his work next day, Scott was furious and said that Fisher had inserted all his own ideas. The result of this clash between two men of strong character was that Fisher left the staff and went to sea again.

Scott was not an easy man to serve. He had been the pioneer of naval gunnery for many years and it is no exaggeration to describe him as a genius. Nearly every apparatus used for training guns' crews was his own invention. He had a remarkable imagination and plenty of drive to force the fruits of his imagination on the service. But he had for many years played a lone hand and, though the time came when he could not be denied and Sir John Fisher and other enlightened senior officers gave him full support, he had at every step met with strong opposition, some of it veiled, and it was this no doubt that made him dictatorial and intolerant when holding the wide powers of the captain of Whale Island. It was also just the moment when his unique position was threatened by other officers who were moving faster than he was in the campaign to develop long-range gunnery; it is quite likely that Fisher, fresh from the *Venerable* firings, did not stick rigidly to his brief. A few years later, Percy Scott had caught up with and passed them, when he solved many baffling problems by his Director firing system.

Fisher wrote, "I feel he means to ruin me", but he now enjoyed a reputation in the service which could weather minor storms, and Admiral Sir William May and his flag captain, A. C. Leveson, were quick to seize the chance of obtaining his services as first and gunnery lieutenant of the new Atlantic Fleet flagship, the *King Edward VII*.

He took up his new appointment in January, 1905.

The next eighteen months were some of the busiest of his career. The *King Edward VII* class mounted a mixed armament of 12″, 9.2″, and 6″ guns, and controlling this armament at long range was the most difficult task that fell to a gunnery officer of that day.

The torpedo lieutenant now played an important part in striving after gunnery efficiency, as the control of the broadside was effected through a maze of electrical instruments and a fault in one of them could cause disaster as there was no time to discover and remedy a defect in the few minutes allowed for a practice shoot. A. D. P. R. Pound was the torpedo lieutenant of the *King Edward VII*, and he and Fisher struck up a firm and lasting friendship which, as will be seen later, culminated in a valuable partnership during the Abyssinian Crisis of 1935.

In addition to training the guns' crews for the short-range gunlayer's test, which was still a keenly-contested annual event, and the officers and control numbers for the long-range battle practice, Fisher, being first lieutenant, was the cable officer and responsible for the cleanliness of the mess decks. His hands must have been very full but he, no doubt, enjoyed more than anything taking charge on the forecastle and urging the sailors to beat the other ships at the complicated evolution of mooring ship.

His fine leadership, hard work, and power of quick decision reaped their reward when the *King Edward VII*, though firing at 1000 yards greater range than other battleships, was third at battle practice in the whole Navy. She was just beaten by two ships with less complicated armament, and her officers could with justification claim that their ship had done best of all.

The " Entente Cordiale " was being cemented at this time and Sir William May took his fleet to Brest as part of the celebrations. The officers were entertained royally in Paris and, at the conclusion of the visit, when the special train was about to leave the station, Fisher, having been hoisted on top of his compartment, made an excellent and humorous speech of thanks in French which was greeted with the greatest enthusiasm.

He had another interesting experience at Gibraltar, which is best told in his own words :

We have had a plethora of Royalties. After the Duke of Connaught, came the Queen. She inspected the ship. I was introduced to her. She worked one of our big turret guns and got a " bulls-eye " with the little aiming rifle I attach to it for training the men to shoot. She was quite delightful but deaf, and walked very lame or stiffly. When I told her she made a bull's-eye (of course I had arranged it for her beforehand) she laughed and said, " I didn't do much for that bull's-eye." We lowered her down 30 feet on the hydraulic lift for the wounded in action. It was rather nervous work for me as it had gone wrong once or twice before and fallen down suddenly. It behaved all right this time though. She saw every conceivable thing and at the end photographed us all with her Kodak. I nearly forgot the nicest thing of all. She went to our wireless telegraph and telegraphed to Poldhu, Cornwall, " To the King of England. I am aboard the ship named after you and send you my fondest love." Sniping Henry !

She was cheered by every ship in turn when she left as the Royal Yacht steamed slowly down between the lines of the Fleet. We had grand illuminations one night for her and I dined with the Admiral, and all his family were on board here to see them. The Queen would have stopped on here a good deal longer if Kaiser Bill hadn't been due. She said smilingly to Willy May that " Gibraltar wasn't big enough for both of them, but how sorry she was to leave." Kaiser's advent was sensational. He came in the *Hamburg* with thunders of gun salutes all round him and, in the meanwhile, his attendant Cruiser, the *Friedrich Carl*, quietly rammed the *Prince George*, one of our battleships. The *Prince George* had to be put into dry-dock hurriedly, making a lot of water. The whole thing is rather humorous really—

1. Arrival of Bill.
2. Half sinks a Battleship.
3. Dashes on board *King Edward VII* to find out all he can about our latest ship.
4. Inspects the Rock and sees all the gun positions.
5. Leaves — having done us a good deal of harm and put us to a lot of expense.

With regard to Item 3, I carefully covered with canvas all the fire control instruments and locked the conning tower. They looked awfully sick, but when they asked in broken English why, I said, " No savvy de Lingo."

The first lieutenant of the flagship was one of the few certainties for promotion to commander, but even so, Fisher must have had a thrilling surprise when the signal man brought him the Admiralty message giving the half-yearly promotions for 30th June, 1906. He was only thirty-one and passed over the heads of a large number of lieutenants. Leveson had recommended him very strongly and in his report said, " He is a leader of men and has a way of enthusing them very much above the average ", and his recommendation had received the powerful support of the Commander-in-Chief. Far from Percy Scott's " ruining him ", he was a commander at least six months earlier than he would have been if he had remained at Whale Island.

CHAPTER V

1906-1912

Commander, H.M.S. *Albemarle*, Atlantic Fleet — Commander, H.M.S. *Indomitable*, for Royal Visit to Canada — Flag Commander, Home Fleet — Flag Commander to Commander-in-Chief, Plymouth — Marriage — Promoted to Captain

FISHER was the ideal executive officer (as the commander was called) of a big ship, as he was not only a leader of men and able to infect officers and men with his enthusiasm for efficiency, but he was also one of the acknowledged leaders in the new gunnery crusade.

It may seem strange that at that period in development an executive officer's interest in the armament should have been in any way noteworthy but though, as we have seen, a large number of senior officers had been seized with the importance of the new and startling changes and had been carried along with the wave of enthusiasm, there was still a considerable number who took very slight interest in the gunnery training and did little or nothing to help the gunnery lieutenant, and in a few cases hindered him.

Though Lord Fisher had begun to concentrate our naval strength in home waters and had paid off a large number of small vessels of little fighting value, many of the commanders had spent much of their career in the backwaters, where the annual firings were often looked on as something to be got through with as little fuss as possible. Good seamen all, they were keen for their men to be smart when paraded as small-arm companies and eager for their ship to take a high place in the Annual

Musketry Course, but they looked on the main armament as the special province of the gunnery officer and the new control contraptions as black magic.

They had been brought up to regard the executive officer of a ship as a superior being whose every whim had to be indulged and who, when telling off the crew for work, might sometimes meet the requests of the gunnery and torpedo lieutenants for men to train for battle, but as often as not refused their requests because there was, in his opinion, more important work to be done — holystoning the decks, cleaning the bright-work, refitting and training in boats and seamanship. So they not only found difficulty in understanding all that was going forward in the gunnery world, but did not take at all kindly to the new order which compelled them to give priority to the requests of the gunnery lieutenant and keep in subjection their own desire to give priority to beautifying the ship and her boats.

Serious clashes between commanders and the gunnery officers were not infrequent and the latter could not always look for support to their captain, who, though a fine seaman bred in the sailing era, was often too old and set to attune his mind to the rapidly changing and somewhat bewildering conditions.

It should not be inferred that these officers were lacking in loyalty or had not the interests of the service at heart. They had given their all from the day they had joined the Navy. It was the old story of men belonging to a profession the customs and methods of which, after long usage, seem to them inviolate, being faced suddenly with drastic innovations. There was nothing reprehensible in their attitude ; they honestly believed that the reformers, unless kept in check, would rob the service of something it could not afford to lose if it was still to remain the finest service in the world.

There was some reason on their side. Before long

some of the gunnery enthusiasts were postulating that the choice lay between gunnery efficiency and "brightwork", because there was not time for both. That, fortunately, died a quick death when the ships that were the smartest and cleanest and best at evolutions were always at the top in the gunlayer's test and battle practice, which was quite natural, as success at anything sprang from the same cause — good leadership.

So a ship, and particularly the gunnery officer, was fortunate when her commander was right up to date.

Fisher had not long to wait for his first appointment as commander. He joined the *Albemarle* in September, 1906. She was the flagship of the Rear-Admiral Atlantic Fleet, and during his year and nine months in her, she wore the flags of Rear-Admirals G. C. Egerton and J. R. Jellicoe.

He soon realised that difficult days lay ahead. The ship was not in good order; the discipline left much to be desired; and the ship's record at coaling, evolutions, and gunnery practice was a poor one.

A few years earlier "coal ship" had become an evolution and, when the Fleet was ordered to coal, all ships vied with one another for the highest average tons per hour taken on board. Commanders now made or marred their reputation on the coaling-performance of their ship, because a good coaling was only possible when the men responded whole-heartedly to good leadership, when the organisation was very thorough and when the many whips and guys and derricks were rigged by a good seaman.

Fisher soon made himself felt. It was an uphill task, but by October he had discovered and purged the ship of the men who were at the root of the indiscipline. He was forced to use a heavy hand during the first few weeks and had to allay his captain's anxiety when the entries in the punishment return bounded up:

The Captain spoke to me rather seriously about the enormous number of punishments I have to give the men. You see they are all officially recorded. I gave him my views of the situation as I found it, as it was now, and how I hoped it would be in another month. He rather winced, but he's such a good chap he didn't mind and I think felt it's going to be all right, though from the questions he asked me he was evidently frightened about the men's attitude to me. They'll be grand in a short time.

And they were. The *Albemarle* sprang into activity under Fisher's wise and virile leadership and was soon at the top in every competitive exercise instead of being at the bottom. To his delight, Captain R. F. Scott (of Antarctic fame) took command of the ship in January, and Fisher was serving again under a man who, holding similar views on discipline and the standard to be achieved, gave him full support.

A little later, when Jellicoe hoisted his flag in the ship, both officers and men were inspired to make a supreme effort. " With Jellicoe ", Fisher wrote, " one doesn't like anything to be second-rate or ill-considered, because he has never failed and has always been successful."

In June he wrote :

I shall have no time to write either tonight or tomorrow. We start at daybreak to get in 1700 tons of coal which is a tremendous business. We are now preparing for it. I am going to try to make more reputation for the ship tomorrow. Rapid coaling is what the C-in-C is most keen on. We shan't finish until about 10 at night, — pretty well dead, I expect.

When Captain Scott was relieved by Captain W. E. Goodenough in August, 1907, Scott wrote in glowing terms of all that his commander had achieved :

A first-rate executive officer with exceptional tact and ability in handling men. The great improvement which has taken place in the shooting, the drills, and the appearance of the ship during the last eight months, I consider to be mainly, if not wholly, due to this officer.

Two extracts from his letters are the best evidence that, despite his heavy preoccupation with restoring discipline, smartening-up the ship and her boats, organising the ship's company for drills, and coaling, his enthusiasm for gunnery efficiency never abated.

Before the gunlayers' test he wrote :

This year the target is a ¼ of the size of last year so that scores will be much lower. I've been talking hot air and fussing round generally and I think we may make a show. So far the *Caesar* is top ship with 52 hits v.g.i. We *must* beat 52 ! We shall perhaps fire on Tuesday, 26th March (MY BIRTHDAY). Good omen !

After the battle practice he wrote :

The Battle Practice was of course a grand eight minutes of life. I controlled the fore turret (12 inch guns) Dannreuther the 6″, and Jeffreys (1st lieutenant) the after 12 inch turret.

I opened the ball and my shot fell short which I meant it to and then fired 6 more, each one crashing through the target. My record stood at 7 rounds, 6 hits. Jeffreys fired his rounds and got one hit or two. Umpires only allowed one but I think he got two. Dannreuther fired 96 six inch shots with 29 hits. After two minutes our target was a shambles and nearly all succeeding shots went through the wrecked part and we got no credit for them, but we got the trophy which now has *Albemarle* as well as *King Edward VII* on it. The Commander-in-Chief who was leading signalled, " I thank *Albemarle* for a splendid exhibition ". I thought we had about 60 hits. Never mind we were top, and in nightfiring we were top, and for all our firings we have had an Admiralty letter of appreciation, and yesterday we beat the record at coaling which is the hardest, most sustained, bit of work any ship does. The C-in-C signalled " Coaling brilliantly executed ".

No wonder Captain Goodenough reported, " Commander Fisher is an officer whom both officers and men will follow anywhere ".

He had come brilliantly through the most difficult task that falls to a naval officer, restoring discipline and enthusiasm and efficiency in a ship that had fallen into slack ways and was far below standard in every undertaking.

His selection as commander of the *Indomitable*, fitting out to take the Prince of Wales to Canada, came as no surprise. He joined her in June, 1908.

Preparing the ship was a rush job and he had to keep the ship's company at work till ten or eleven at night. The redoubtable Jacky Fisher, now First Sea Lord, visited the ship on the morning she sailed and was delighted with all he saw. He came with twenty cadets, amongst them Prince Edward, and was much amused when one of the cadets said to him, " I see you've arranged to have a relative as commander of the *Indomitable* ".

The Prince of Wales, who had served many years afloat, was also quick to appreciate what Fisher had done in such a short time. " The Prince came up to me in a very friendly way and said, ' What beautiful paint you've put on ! ' For which I blessed him."

He was bidden to dine with the Royal party on the first evening and after dinner, when talking to Sir F. Hopwood and Lord Annaly, could hardly keep awake. " I was absolutely worn out and I really do confess it — perhaps not with work but tension." The Prince was playing bridge, but his keen eye detected that the commander was dead tired and he sent a message that he was not to stand on ceremony but go when he liked.

Royal passengers are a heavy responsibility for the captain, and the commander has his own special anxieties as he is responsible for their well-being and the ship's specially high standard of smartness and cleanliness on arrival in port, whatever the weather experienced on passage. Their luck was out, for the ship ran into heavy weather on the second day and not only did an enforced reduction of speed jeopardise the chance of arriving at Quebec at the scheduled time — so important for a Royal visit — but a lot of water was shipped and penetrated into the Royal cabins.

Later on the captain had many anxious hours when fog and icebergs were encountered. The engine-room complement was not large enough for the continual high-speed steaming and Fisher had to detach a considerable number of seamen to work as stokers and he himself took turns in the stokehold.

This reduction in the upper-deck complement and the bad weather spelt ruin to the enamel paint and gold leaf and Fisher's hopes of arriving at Quebec spick and span were dashed.

Nothing, however, could damp his high spirits and as soon as the gale subsided he was persuading the Royal suite to take part in deck games. " We had them all up to deck cricket and other naval games such as ' Sling the monkey ' and ' Bait the bear '. The Prince came up and roared with laughter when I caught Dudley a terrific smack on his fat sides."

The Royal visit to Canada lasted only seven days, and there was great excitement about the passage home, as it was hoped the *Indomitable* would win the Blue Riband for the fastest Atlantic crossing. So keen was everyone on board that all hands, including the Prince, took a turn in the stokehold. She averaged 25.13 knots and just beat the *Lusitania*'s record.

The King and Queen went on board when the ship anchored off Cowes and the King was delighted when he learnt from Commodore King-Hall that his commander was a son of his old tutor and private secretary. " He simply beamed all over and said, ' What? Do you mean to say you are the son of my old friend, Herbert

Fisher?'" Fisher and the engineer and navigating commanders were given the M.V.O.; four of the hardest-working stokers were given the Victorian Medal and received it begrimed and barefooted and straight from their work.

His friend, Maurice Baring, was his guest when the *Indomitable* went on an independent cruise to Spanish waters after the Royal tour and was a great favourite in the ship:

> We gave Baring a great dinner last night. He made two speeches; the second he called a "postscript". We sang "For he's a jolly good fellow" and drank his health very often. It's extraordinary the hold he has got on all hands from the Cook's Mate to the Commander! We are dreadfully sorry he is going tonight. He has been the life of the mess.

That was the first of Maurice Baring's many cruises with Fisher, who, whenever he was afloat, pressed Baring to join him.

Fisher's next appointment as Flag Commander to the Commander-in-Chief Home Fleet opened up a new field of work under his old chief, Sir William May, who flew his flag in the *Dreadnought*, the all-big-gun ship that Jacky Fisher had created and had built in an astonishingly short time, and which caused a considerable stir amongst naval officers and ship designers all over the world.

Owing to the immense increase in gunnery activity, it had become impossible for the gunnery lieutenant of the flagship to deal with all the paper work, returns, and firing programmes, and a commander experienced in gunnery matters was now appointed to the staffs of Commanders-in-Chief with the title of Flag Commander.

It was a coveted appointment, as the holders were able to exercise great influence on the progress of the gunnery and the Commander-in-Chief looked to his Flag Commander for advice on every aspect of armament training and he became the friend and adviser of all the gunnery lieutenants.

Though great advances had been made in the art of long-range firing there was still a large field for further exploration and Fisher had little leisure during his two years on the staff.

It was not, however, his gunnery work that made this a remarkable period in his career ; it was his association with Sir William May in the study and solution of tactical problems.

In a very few years the effective battle range had doubled and the main fleets were growing rapidly in numbers, and cruisers, fitted with wireless telegraphy, could now give the Commander-in-Chief early information of the enemy's numbers, formation, course, and speed. As it took a considerable time for a fleet to manœuvre from a cruising formation into the long single battle line, which enabled all ships to bring their broadsides to bear on the enemy, the Commander-in-Chief's object was to deploy his fleet early and also correctly, so that when both fleets were in battle line his ships would engage their targets under favourable conditions of sun and wind with all guns able to fire. The latter was an important point as the arcs of the guns were limited by upper-deck structures.

This was not, of course, an entirely new field of exploration ; mimic battles were a regular feature in the programme of every fleet, but now the time had come to approach the whole problem afresh and scientifically.

Fisher's original mind was of great assistance to Sir William May, whilst he was carrying out an exhaustive series of deployments under all conditions of weather and on various assumptions with regard to the enemy's first reported position, course, and speed. When completed and analysed, the lessons learned became the foundations of modern Fleet Tactics.

Sir William May was very grateful to Fisher and wrote, " A most able and capable officer in every way. Commander Fisher's knowledge of Naval Tactics and gunnery is quite exceptional."

Fisher was thus present at two epoch-marking series of trials — the *Venerable* trials, which established principles for long-range firing, and the Home Fleet trials, which established principles of tactics for an age of fast, powerfully armed ships, equipped with wireless telegraphy.

King Edward VII died when the Fleet was in Campbeltown, during a Scottish cruise, and Fisher was very indignant at the way the news was received and the lack of imagination and respect shown by some of the senior officers and parsons:

I went for a walk with the Admiral from 2 to 4, a lovely walk over the hills and I enjoyed it so much. I think we both felt how little many people seem to realise what had happened. Even in our own Service where the men seemed to go about their work and laugh and skylark as if it was quite an ordinary thing to lose the King they served. As far as I know no Captain made any special reference to his men, and this to me is hardly comprehensible, for I feel sure they would have been so ready to listen. Nothing grand or solemn has been done barring the firing of minute guns and I long to be an ordinary Commander to have men and to join issue with them as brothers who have lost a parent.

This morning I felt I couldn't go to Church in the *Dreadnought*, though the Admirals and the others did. I went ashore to the Scotch Church. In the *Dreadnought* the parson made no allusion whatever to the King. He turned on the ordinary meaningless stuff he happened to have prepared.

In the *Bellerophon* F. Larken tells me there was worse, however — the congregation of " sailors " were asked to be " charitable " in their thoughts for the dead monarch.

I was glad I went ashore for Church for I found myself closely penned in by others who felt as I did.

I like the solemn straightforward earnest Scottish Service. Nearly everyone was crying and at the end the Dead March was played and all stood up. One poor little girl of about 11 who was looking after a Ros of two couldn't hold herself in and I wanted to tell her she needn't be ashamed of giving way. We got out of the Church in beautiful sunshine and I saw all her spirits come back — which was abs: right."

The Fleet was ordered to Kingstown so that representatives from the Fleet could take part in the memorial service at St. Patrick's Cathedral in Dublin; Fisher's account of the proceedings contains a striking tribute to his Commander-in-Chief:

Eventually arrived and moved slowly up the aisle. Without any exaggeration and it is what I've heard from others on shore, Willy May made everyone else look absolutely commonplace. Although I see him every day I was absolutely carried away! It was most remarkable — his whole expression and bearing just right for the particular occasion. The Navy made a very good show.

But he thought the service very poor:

The general impression left on my mind was that the service might have almost served for any other occasion. No dirges or solemn word and much coughing everywhere, showing lack of emotion. My little Presbyterian Church at Campbeltown did better!

His affection and deep respect for his Admiral moved him to great indignation over the press reports on an important strategical exercise which, based on wrong information, gave the victory to Prince Louis of Battenberg, who was Sir William May's opponent.

A friend, in fun, wrote to him, "Why didn't you acknowledge to me that Red Fleet has been beaten instead of writing all that stuff about its resounding to Willy May's credit?"

Great Guffin! [he replied] When you've read my explanation you'll see that we're not such asses as we look.

(1) The whole exercise was constructed by us and we

could have thwarted Prince Louis any moment we liked, though to give our Cruiser Admirals and lookouts practice we told them nothing.

(2) Not one ship of Blue Fleet got anywhere near the Forth Bridge or Rosyth.

(3) The whole operations were completely successful for . . . RED ! !

(4) Everything " has redounded ", etc. etc. ! !

Now how does this all come into the papers. Aye, there's the rub ! !

He goes on to explain that Prince Louis, as a joke, made a signal *en clair* that he had destroyed the Forth Bridge and Rosyth, and finished with another tribute to his Commander-in-Chief :

The whole programme has gone without a hitch. Every date and hour have been kept. Perfectly orderly and thought-out. W. H. M.'s bringing his mighty Armada into Scapa Flow opened a good many eyes.

In the spring of 1911 Sir William May was appointed Commander-in-Chief, Plymouth, and asked Fisher to continue with him as Flag Commander.

A home port Flag Commander's work was not onerous and for the first time Fisher enjoyed a period of comparative leisure.

Whilst in the *Albemarle* he had married Cecilia, youngest daughter of Mr. Francis Warre Cornish, a brilliant scholar and Vice-Provost of Eton.

Mr. Warre Cornish was a successful and much-beloved teacher and a leader of thought at Eton and was the author of some important works, including *Jane Austen* for the English Men of Letters Series, a comprehensive *History of the Church of England in the Nineteenth Century*, a Dictionary of Antiquities, and a *Life of Oliver Cromwell*.

His wife was a daughter of the Hon. W. Ritchie, legal member of the Council in India, and sister of Sir Richmond Ritchie, who married Thackeray's daughter.

The Fishers took a house about four miles out of Plymouth. These were halcyon days. Though a " son of Anak ", Fisher's highly-strung nature must have been constantly under strain during the long years of striving to place his ship at the top in the gunlayers' test and battle practice, and later, as commander, at the top in coaling and evolutions; the change to a peaceful life must have been very welcome. He loved his bicycle rides to and from his work, played a lot of tennis, and got immense enjoyment in the company of his small daughter, " Ros ".

After nine months at Plymouth he was appointed to the new battle cruiser *Princess Royal*, which was approaching completion. For six months he superintended her fitting out, but before she commissioned he was promoted to captain, on 1st July, 1912. He was then thirty-seven and a half, which was unusually young for promotion, but though he passed over the heads of a large number of commanders, no one grudged him his quick advancement. It was recognised that he had earned it, that he was worthy of it and that it was for the benefit of the Navy.

ADMIRAL SIR W. H. MAY AND STAFF, H.M.S. *DREADNOUGHT*
Flag-Commander Fisher standing behind Admiral

FLAG-CAPTAIN, H.M.S. *ST. VINCENT*

CHAPTER VI

1912-1918

Captain, H.M.S. *St. Vincent*, Grand Fleet — Battle of Jutland — Director of Anti-submarine Division, Admiralty

FISHER did not have to wait long for his first command. The Fleet was expanding rapidly and the long periods of unemployment for senior officers, which bore so heavily on the married men and sometimes blunted their enthusiasm, were now a thing of the past.

On 10th December, 1912, he was appointed to the battleship *St. Vincent*, wearing the flag of Rear-Admiral Gough-Calthorpe, and remained in command of her for three years and five months.

After a year, Rear-Admiral Evan Thomas succeeded Gough-Calthorpe, but early in 1916 the *St. Vincent* became a private ship and so Fisher became by many years the youngest captain in command of a capital ship, other than a flagship — striking recognition by Sir John Jellicoe and the Admiralty of his outstanding qualities. After the first few days of the commission he was able to write that everything was going well:

Lovely sunny morning. Feel very much on the ball as I can see that we are making a good start and that Dudley Pound is a treasure, no "humming or hawing" over any suggestion of mine. The slightest wish is carried out to the fullest. So I have *great hopes*. Now imagine my day such as it generally is. Diving into a turret and gingering-up the officers and men here and showing that I know every detail, then to the ship's galley to see the food cooked, then to the bakery, then to the boiler room to see the stokers at work, then a hand-on-arm to wireless operator, Sick Bay, Carpenters — inspected the boys (56 all told) — arranged their instruction. Got out programme for Team Marathon races — arranged a cricket match, officers and men, this afternoon. This always produces an excellent impression early in a commission. Then organised their choir practice to be held every night at 6.30. It was a great success last night.

That was always his way. Filling every minute of the day, just as eager that every department in his ship should be at the highest standard of efficiency as he was about a cricket match or the prospect of a long tramp over the hills.

Those were strenuous days in the Home Fleet. The Kaiser was increasing the tempo of his shipbuilding and there was now no disguising that he and his advisers would set their great war-machine in motion as soon as the time was ripe. Greater and still greater efforts to increase battle-worthiness were demanded from officers and men of the great Fleet commanded by Admiral Sir George Callaghan. For the next twenty months Fisher was caught up in this whirl of activity, always striving for a still higher standard; when war was declared on 4th August, 1914, the *St. Vincent* was at the highest pitch of all-round efficiency. Her officers and men had the utmost confidence in their inspiring captain, and he in them:

Tonight the Ward Room are dining the Warrant officers and I hear snatches of songs. Good fellows all of them and I should like to have the chance of seeing their behaviour in action. *Not one* that I can't trust to the bitter bitter end.

Life at Scapa Flow, which was the main base, has often been described. The effort to increase efficiency was never relaxed, though as the months passed without a sight of a German man-of-war, many doubted if the great main fleets would ever meet in battle. The health and welfare of the vast community living under abnormal conditions was a principal concern of the Commander-in-Chief and his senior officers, and every kind of athletic pursuit was encouraged. It was a time when good leadership was of great importance. There was no tennis and no racquets now, but Fisher seldom missed a chance of a ramble over the countryside, when the Fleet was not at short notice for steam :

So W. W. goes by himself with a grin like a crack in a pie and takes the " dawg ". Oilskins on. Along, along, along the good muddy roads, sniffing rank turnip fields, peering into reeking damp cottage windows and finally standing on some cliffs inhaling deep breaths of the Atlantic and trying to gaze through the fog for a possible " grey cigar ". The dog was splendid company. I sent him after seagulls and larks, and hid from him like I do from Ros and Ra. It was very jolly to be alone — to go one's own pace and think one's own thoughts.

And sometimes the senior officers would meet on shore and he would enjoy a talk with them :

To a hill-top (two-mile walk solo in sun over heather to get there) where Leveson had tea ready — found an august company. George Hope of *Queen Elizabeth* ; Phillpotts of *Warspite* ; Seymour of *Centurion* ; Admirals Sturdee, Halsey, and finally the Commander-in-Chief himself. So I was well pleased. Dear little J. coming up with his winning smile and shaking hands all round. When we all went off, I strode away by myself for a thorough good quiet time. The few cornfields were green, other fields bright yellow with mustard — some of the ground hard and rough as Gallipoli — but where it was so were the most beautiful small wild flowers. I send Ros and Racy one wild pansy each. Plenty of Ros's and Racy's playing about in the evening sun — found one such happy party — three little girls and a tiny Nevil, all hay-making ; poor little crofter's children, barefooted, home an Irish cabin. I said, " If the man of the party is brave enough to come to me, he'll get a present." No, he wouldn't, his white hair shone in the sun, all fluffy. The little girls tried to make him. No. So I put the present (which was a shilling) on the post of a gate which I thought he could *just* reach, and then I walked away about thirty yards and saw the delicious sight of the little fellow toddle gravely across all by himself, tiptoe up and feel the shilling and get it. Looked at it carefully and very thoughtfully, took it back and showed it to his sisters, who didn't snatch it from him but let him keep it — the dear little fellow, so like Nevil — well, you see what a blubber-hearted old whale I am now I'm a father.

The welfare of his officers and men was a constant preoccupation and he was always devising something new to amuse them and keep them fit :

Today found us unexpectedly motionless. Opposite some undulating country deep in snow. I send for old Pilch [Pilcher, the Commander] and say, " A treasure hunt this evening for all the midshipmen and any sailors who care." I go ashore at 1.30 with a tin box and 10 bob inside it. We arranged a course of about seven miles over hill and burn. Most of the clues were in crofters' huts and they entered into it like one o'clock, especially the women. The wind-up was at the village school where the last clue was given : " Seek the prettiest in the village, encircle her waist and you will find the treasure." Great brain-wave this of mine. The schoolmaster larfed a lot and said, " You must go to Barbara Muir at the Mill ! " Romantic ! Fair freckled Barbara, quite game, and put the tin box in her bosom. We then sped back to meet the party landing at 4.15. A splendid muster. 50 men and 12 mids — off they went. Whilst I cut across waiting to see the sequel in the village. My crikey, you would have larfed. Sailors diving into houses calling for all the girls and " waisting " them, others shy. And then a girl rides through on a bicycle and can't understand why 20 pursue her. Laughs and draws them on for two miles. At last Barbara is found and the whole countryside cheer. They've a lot to talk about in their messes tonight — the whole thing was a rare lark.

That was the true Fisher touch.

He was always busy, but like all his brother officers at Scapa he sometimes longed to be in the fighting in the more distant seas.

All is well and we must play the part that the old sailors did 100 years ago when they watched for three years off Brest or Toulon. It does make one's mouth water when we read of exciting times for our ships in all parts of the world under warm suns. Don't imagine we are doing nothing. *Just the reverse.* Had a long talk with J. R. J. this morning — also with Madden. Tremendous sense of confidence everywhere in them, in ourselves (conceited this), our ships and planes. For short, it is splendid to be English — isn't it? Everyone ready to put all personal considerations aside for the good of the Country.

He was intensely interested in tactics and frequently forwarded the results of his investigations to the flagship. He brought his fertile imagination to bear on all the difficult problems that arose through the inactivity of the German main Fleet and the growing power of the German submarines.

In December he worked out in detail a plan for an offensive operation in the Heligoland Bight with the object of destroying Heligoland Dockyard and enticing heavy ships from Cuxhaven or Wilhelmshaven. In the covering letter is an example of his generous mind: "Commander Pound has considered this question with me. Indeed he is responsible for anything of any value that these suggestions may contain."

After Jutland he wrote a masterly paper on the submarine menace, in which he urged that the development of the hydroplane should be pushed on with all speed, and made detailed proposals, including the name of every ship to be employed, for sealing and keeping sealed the channels used by the submarines in the Jade, the Weser, and the Elbe, and also the three Baltic exits, the Sound, Great Belt, and Little Belt. His plan included mines and block-ships, and also spike-ships for shallow waters.

The Commander-in-Chief made frequent use of his gunnery knowledge and put him on most of the committees that dealt with armament questions. He was the originator of a scheme for eliminating vertical lines by fitting iron triangles to edges and masts so as to render range-finding by the enemy more difficult.

He was instrumental in starting a scheme for the officers of the Fleet to meet periodically to discuss fighting methods. He had absolute faith in the Commander-in-Chief:

> I see the C-in-C quite often and am struck every time with his marvellous alertness and precision. Rather commonplace sort of description of him — but it's correct. No unsound however attractive proposal has a rabbit's chance when he turns his searchlight brain on it — it's riddled by a dry fact or two that he knows but that no one else seems to.

Fisher evoked loyalty and high service from his officers and men and was always extremely loyal to them. When his gunnery lieutenant, J. S. M. Ritchie, fell ill, he would not hear of another gunnery lieutenant being appointed, though pressed by his squadron Admiral to apply for one.

> Make your mind perfectly easy about the ship [he wrote] : your department has been so organised that it can run without you for many weeks, but I won't have a new broom upsetting things and upsetting me. The Bosches will wait for you all right.

And in another letter :

> Don't worry if they put you back for a week or so, get really strong whilst you are about it. The above are my orders (which you may not obey), also my wishes (which you must consider). We had our full calibre full charge Director shoot last Monday. Someone will have told you of it and all the comic sideshows that were enacted. Only three people proved themselves asses, 1st class, viz. : — Captain, who gave one or two ridiculous spotting corrections. . . .

No wonder officers and men loved serving with him. He always adopted a policy of persuasion and example with officers who faltered in their duty. He instituted a Debating Society in the wardroom to pass away the long evenings and started community singing for the sailors. He also gave frequent lectures to the ship's company:

> Am getting a lecture ready for the men — shall fire it off tonight perhaps, being an unexpected quiet evening, "British sailors in action." Collected a good many stories old and new and can put in some padding to cheer them up. I'm always so afraid of enthusiasm dwindling. It is hard to keep it up to top note. I can, but I wouldn't if I allowed myself to drift off into novels and gentle lines of thought. I'm sure that's fatal.

His restless and original brain was always devising some new scheme to counter boredom and keep everyone happy, with the result that the ship always took a high place in her squadron at coaling and shone in the many competitions, ashore and afloat.

The long wait ended in the last week of May, 1916, when the Commander-in-Chief received news that the German Fleet was stirring. He proceeded at once to sea with his great armada in the hopes of at last bringing the enemy to battle. This is not the place to re-tell the oft-told story of the battle of Jutland. Fisher, being captain of a battleship, was never fully engaged but his letter, written two days after return to harbour, is of interest as it shows that he appreciated at the time Jellicoe's masterly handling of the situation. The battle being indecisive, as the German commander had no intention of fighting, raised a storm of controversy about Jellicoe's tactics. Writers, who had little or no knowledge of sea war, entered the lists and aired their views on the right tactics for the particular condition of low visibility and an enemy of at least equal speed.

It was some years before the controversy died down and it was the demonstration of the battle at the Tactical

School at Portsmouth, attended at some time by most senior officers, that finally sealed Jellicoe's reputation as a master tactician. Fisher wrote:

Charles [his brother] and I were on shore together having the greatest fun when recalled, as we have been recalled dozens of times before. Exactly twenty-four hours later the *St. Vincent* steamed past the wreck of a ship which we took to be a German. We were, with other ships near us in the line, engaging four German Dreadnoughts at the time, but I looked to see if there was anyone in the water near this ship and saw nothing — not even floating wreckage. All round was still calm water. The wreck might have been there for weeks — and yet we know now she went down only about a quarter of an hour before our arrival. Her bow was high in the air and so was her stern, the centre having been split in two and apparently resting on the bottom. She was turned more over than I have drawn it, so that one saw her keel and so couldn't recognise the ship, but we know now that she was the *Invincible*. Our advanced guard of Battle Cruisers got into action about an hour and a half before the main fleet and it was then that all our losses occurred — or nearly all. The weather was most unfortunately hazy — ships only visible about 10,000 yards, which for our modern guns is next to point blank. And so I suppose that through not being able to see the full enemy forces they came unexpectedly under the fire of fresh battle divisions and were too proud to withdraw till we came up. The sight when we arrived was unforgettable. The heavy roll of broadsides, and then their flame through the grey mist, and then our ships ploughing past with towering splashes all round them. They gave way to let us through but even then it was very hard to see the enemy — occasionally seeing one, then in another place three or four or five as the patches of haze varied. And of course at our end of the line the view was different to what it was at the centre or head who were opposite different enemy ships whom we couldn't see. It was clear that the Commander-in-Chief had put us in the most wonderful position. At our end a few broadsides disposed of a biggish cruiser who sank in about five minutes, and then, being in such a good position, we could not help overwhelming three battleships of the *Kaiser* class who were opposite us. Their fire got wilder and slower and it is fairly established that one was sunk. They turned away after half an hour and some of their destroyers cleverly came between us and them, making a heavy pall of smoke which hid them completely. By now the whole Fleet was steering towards Heligoland to catch them again. Destroyers and Submarines made attacks on our end, a good many torpedoes coming close, the ship astern of me being hit but not giving in to it, though I was alarmed for her. Night came on and all round the horizon there were the searchlights, flashes and bursts of flame as shells got home. Impossible to make out what was happening, but the principal thing was repeated attacks of our Destroyers on the scattered divisions of their Battle Fleet. From all the evidence I think the Commander-in-Chief is certain that two German battleships were blown up. We all saw two enormous explosions at the times stated by the Destroyers, and no big ship of ours suffered after 7.15 P.M. A very cold raw morning and still misty found us in very dangerous waters, probably heavily mined and with every submarine that could be summoned or sent to sea in a position to attack us. Visibility about two miles only. We cast East and West and North and then South again, but they were behind their known minefields and a couple of Zeppelins was all we saw. The German first announcement is of course quite untrue. As we had so far to go to get back and we did not all go back to the same place, it has taken time to find out all that was done. But the German losses are far heavier than they will ever admit, and I am afraid will put their Battle Fleet in such relative inferiority to ours, which is untouched, that we shall not get another chance. The inability to see more than small parts of the picture at a time which deprives one of the powers of meeting their tactics, and the fact that we had only two hours of daylight, caused us to miss the sort of result we have dreamt of for so long. The sort of action that we *have* to accept is bound to be costly. It is almost like playing a man with loaded dice. He knows very well that if he comes out a respectable distance (and in this case he was so very close to the coast all the time) we shall certainly go for him, and with his submarines and mines he can dispose the pieces on the board on a cut-and-dried plan to his great advantage. Admiral Jellicoe seems to have avoided all these dangers in a wonderful way.

Fisher's admiration for Jellicoe, the man, is shown in a letter he wrote at this period on religion and faith :

> To bolster up a double-dyed ass like myself, I think of the great people who have been entirely satisfied with the New Testament, Tennyson, Garibaldi, Thomas Hardy, Nelson, Lord Roberts, Jellicoe — our beloved Commander-in-Chief, the finest character that ever was.

The loss of his brother, Charles, who was serving in the *Invincible* as a lieutenant, R.N.V.R., after strenuous service in France, was a very severe blow to him. He was deeply attached to his brother and whenever the *Invincible* and *St. Vincent* were in company, the two brothers could be seen striding over the moors in the highest spirits or getting an immense amount of fun over a game of golf on the links on Flotta Island, which had been carved out of unpromising land by the officers of the Fleet. He wrote :

> I am comforted by the knowledge that he who had seen so much carnage will have steadied everyone near him. How proud I have been to walk about as Charles's brother, and prouder, if possible, than ever now. But how impossible to be like him.

The poignant memory of that quarter of an hour, between the time he realised it was the wreck of the *Invincible* and he closed his binoculars knowing he would never see his brother again, remained vivid to the end of his life.

There was much food for serious thought when the reports from the senior officers had been examined. There were two most disturbing facts — our ships had blown up after very slight punishment and the German ships that had been heavily punished had survived. The efficiency of our shells was under grave suspicion and when the matter was thoroughly explored, those suspicions were shown to be only too well founded. Fisher was not concerned with that problem, as he had never had any connection with the manufacture of ammunition, which was the province of the Controller, the Director of Naval Ordnance, and the Ordnance Committee.

The vulnerability of our ships to slight punishment was, on the other hand, a matter for action on the spot and Jellicoe at once set up a strong Committee, which included Fisher, to probe into everything and anything that would throw light on the cause of the disasters. There were no survivors from the *Indefatigable*, and only a few from the *Queen Mary*, who had by a miracle escaped from the after part of the ship, but the evidence of the gunnery officer of the *Invincible*, who had a remarkable escape, threw some light on what had happened, and very important information was brought to the Committee by officers of the *Lion*, Beatty's flagship, which, but for the presence of mind of two officers who ordered the magazine doors to be closed, would have met the same fate as her consorts.

Fisher's reasoning powers and great knowledge of guns and their mountings was a source of strength to the Committee and, working at high speed, an agreed report on what must be done at once was rendered to the Commander-in-Chief. The principal recommendation was a drastic change of system at the stage when the cordite was being passed out of the magazines, a change which necessitated alteration to the magazine doors and the ship being out of action whilst the work was being done.

It was typical of Fisher that, when the orders were issued allowing six days for the work, he at once decided that the *St. Vincent* would be completed in three and a half days. As it was work beyond the capacity of the ship's artisans, skilled dockyard employees had to be brought north and it was these men whom Fisher had to inspire to work hard for long hours. They could not resist his appeal and the work was completed in three and a half days.

Another matter that required careful investigation was our method of controlling the fire of the broadsides on first engaging an enemy, as it had been evident that at Jutland the Germans had been more successful at obtaining early hits than we had. Fisher played an important part in revising our methods.

Whilst these strenuous efforts were being made to profit from the lessons of the first meeting between the main fleets, the war took a very ugly turn for us. In September, 1916, the German submarines sank 104,500 tons of our merchant shipping and, by December, the figure had risen to 182,000 tons. As Jellicoe expressed it — "The submarines are bleeding us to death." In November, Jellicoe attended a full-dress meeting at the Admiralty and suggested that a Flag Officer with wide powers should be appointed to the Admiralty to take charge of the anti-submarine warfare. During his visit Mr. Balfour asked him if he was prepared to leave the Grand Fleet and cope with the serious menace. Jellicoe consented to do this, because he thought there was very slight chance of the German High Sea Fleet coming out again so as to give the Grand Fleet an opportunity of engaging it, but later on he realised that he would be in a difficult position if working under the Board of Admiralty, and he wrote accordingly to Mr. Balfour. Later in the month he was asked to come to the Admiralty as First Sea Lord. The problem, the most difficult that had ever faced a British Admiralty, had obviously to be tackled by fresh and vigorous minds ; Jellicoe took with him to the Admiralty Rear-Admiral A. L. Duff. Admiral Duff had been supervising trials of the paravane and devices of a similar nature designed to protect ships from mine attack and in his book *The Submarine Peril* Jellicoe describes him as " an officer ever ready to receive and try new ideas and gifted with imagination and great organising ability ".

In his book, *The Foreigner in China*, Mr. O. M. Green has a striking passage about Admiral Duff and Sir Everard Fraser, the Consul-General at Shanghai :

> Two men stand out in memories of China for a quality peculiar to themselves and which I never saw to the same degree in any others — Sir Everard Fraser and Admiral Sir Alexander Duff, who commanded our ships in China from 1919 to 1922. Even at the mere sight of them the Homeric epithet, Agamemnon King of Men, instinctively rose in the mind. There was an indefinable princeliness about them, of which they were no doubt perfectly unaware, but without a trace of condescension. Let me put it this way : no one would have dreamed of taking the slightest liberty with either, but no one would have had the least nervousness in approaching them or any feeling but of easy friendliness in their conversation. There are some rich men who have the happy knack, in entertaining you, of making you feel that you, too, have twenty thousand a year. It was the same, in another sphere, with Sir Everard Fraser and Admiral Duff. They were exactly the same, whomever they were talking with. They were at once grand and disarming.

Admiral Duff was an officer under whom Fisher did some of the most important work of his life. It was his fortune to serve much of his early career under men of " indefinable princeliness " — Sir William May, Sir Alexander Duff, and Sir John de Robeck.

Admiral Duff was first head of the anti-submarine Division, but the extent of the measures at once put in force and those contemplated was soon so great that it was necessary to form several divisions and give the Admiral additional powers by making him a Member of the Board with the title of Assistant Chief of the Naval Staff.

Fisher was appointed Director of the Anti-submarine Division in May, 1917. It was a wrench to him to leave the Fleet and to give up command of the ship of which he was so proud ; but the parting was made easier by his feeling of certainty that the German Fleet would never again give the Grand Fleet a chance of bringing it to battle, and his growing eagerness to be doing something new and more important. He also was beginning to feel the loneliness of his position. Captains always live alone on board, but in peace-time they can go ashore to dine and meet friends or sleep ashore in their own homes. Life at Scapa meant long solitary evenings for the captains and Fisher was a man who loved company and good talk. There had been some talk at an earlier date of an appointment at the Admiralty, but Fisher had then disliked the idea :

Much amused at your endeavour to paint the Admiralty in glowing colours. But just imagine me here the leader of 850 most gallant delightful souls and ready and anxious to keep company with them through whatever the future has in store.

Lord Jellicoe in his letter to the Admiralty, written after the Armistice, bringing to notice the services of the principal officers who had served under him, wrote: " Captain W. W. Fisher, another exceptional officer, whose ship, the *St. Vincent*, was in the very first rank of efficiency ". But now he was not sorry that a new and vitally important field of endeavour had opened out before him.

Fisher brought to his new task qualities which could not be equalled. He had more than two years' experience of war at sea, technical knowledge of a high order, first-rate organising ability, remarkable power of inspiring enthusiasm, a very alert mind, and a capacity for working very long hours without disturbing his own temper.

Lord Fisher was one of the first to express his pleasure. To Captain Fisher he wrote :

Seldom have I had more pleasure than in your succeeding Duff. *Absolutely the right man in the right place.* I always have said the Commander of the *Indomitable* would come out on top. Please bring your wife to lunch here when you get to London. What is her address? I don't forget what I said once that I'd make your wife a widow and your house a dunghill.* But she entertained no malice and sent me a paper I much wished for.

And to Mrs. Fisher

I wrote to your excellent husband to get your address to congratulate you on his being in the *very* forefront of the Battle. Please arrange to bring him here any day you like at 1.30 P.M. I hope to find I shall be useful to him. He has the biggest work of the war, and he'll do it.

Shortly after he started his new work, a friend wrote: " In his usual optimistic way Fisher is raising a whirlwind in the corridors of the Admiralty ".

But perhaps his greatest asset was the ease with which he could discuss problems with scientists and inventors. Enough has already been written to show that his interests were widespread and more varied than those of most naval officers. He was a great reader and it can be inferred, from the account given of his family and his wife's family, that he had always spent his leave in the company of men and women of great and varied attainments. This now stood him in good stead. The scientists appreciated his quick brain and his unfailing courtesy and consideration and, where there might have been clashes of personality, there was full co-operation and there were no delays in pushing on with any promising devices.

This is not the place for a detailed account of that long-drawn-out battle against the submarines. The inner history is only to be found in technical books. The extent of Fisher's activities can, however, be appreciated from

* Lord Fisher was referring, in his forceful style, to his exhortations to the officers of the *Indomitable* to win the Blue Riband of the Atlantic.

a list of some of the offensive measures which he organised. These were hydroplane hunting flotillas ; air patrols requiring aeroplanes, seaplanes, airships, and kite balloons ; submarines specially detailed for anti-submarine operations ; coastal motor-boat hunting flotillas ; decoy ships, both steam and sail ; anti-submarine minefields ; moored hydrophones. Depth-charges and depth-charge throwers and bomb-howitzers had to be developed and large numbers manufactured to meet the requirements of all these new hunting vessels.

Seldom a day passed without Fisher having to weigh up the possibilities of some new invention.

By November, 1917, 2800 vessels were employed in fighting the submarine.

The battle was won, though the situation sometimes looked very black. Slowly but steadily the anti-submarine forces obtained the mastery over their quarry and, by the end of 1917, they were sinking submarines at a rate equivalent to the output of new vessels.

Early in 1918 our output of merchant shipping was in excess of the tonnage being sunk by submarine attack. But perhaps the story of a great achievement is summed up best in Fisher's own notes for a lecture given after the war :

During April with its dreadful average of 10 ships sunk per day, it was obvious that unless some new tide set in, there would be only one end to the war and it would come soon. Think of the cargoes of the ships — food, munitions, ores, textiles. The stupendous waste. The stupendous effort to replace them. No one could definitely say with what minimum tonnage we could still carry on the war. We had about 20 millions at the start. We lost half a million in a single month. Were our total available tonnage reduced to 12 millions it was the general opinion of shipping and trade circles that we should be beaten and long before then that we should have to reduce our scale of effort. By the beginning of 1918, therefore, we might be in a bad way. The situation was gradually redressed and ultimately saved by—

(*a*) The institution of the system of convoy under protection of fighting ships. *Defensive.*

(*b*) The speeding-up of merchant ship building. *Administrative.*

(*e*) The intensification of the war against the U-boats themselves. *Offensive.*

Remembering that in the whole of 1916 we only destroyed 25 U-boats in an average of 2 a month, in—

September	1917, we sank	10	
October	” ”	8	
November	” ”	9	
December	” ”	7	
January	1918 ”	9	
February	” ”	4	very bad weather for small craft
March	” ”	5	
April	” ”	6	
May	” ”	17	*glorious month*

and then a steady average 8 to 10 till the end.

May 1918 was the knock-out blow and there was little heart in the U-boat Commanders after that.

Later on there is this interesting note :

The tracking of the invisible enemy :
Dreams of a solution.
Brains of England and America on it.
In England — Pure Professor, Practical Engineer, Manipulator } the Great Alliance.

Little was known at the time about Fisher's part in this stern battle, which for us was a battle for existence, but when in 1921 Sir Henry Newbolt examined the Admiralty archives, he found what the country owed Fisher and dedicated his *Naval History of the War* to "William Wordsworth Fisher. In the crisis of our fate from June, 1917, to November, 1918, Director of the Anti-submarine Division at the Admiralty."

The American officers, with whom he established the most cordial relations, were full of praise for the help he had given them. The American Force Commander wrote :

At the close of my work on this section, I particularly wish to invite your attention to the hearty co-operation of the Anti-submarine Division of the Admiralty with this section of your staff, without which most of the work accomplished would have been impossible.

The Director of the Anti-submarine Division has at all times shown the greatest interest in American Listening Devices and given us every encouragement and most cheerful and hearty assistance in their development. . . .

I hope in some way the splendid assistance rendered to our Navy in this development work by the Director of the Anti-submarine Division of the Admiralty and the above officers may receive some recognition from our Government.

This chapter can fittingly close with a letter written to Fisher, shortly after the Armistice, by one of the leading scientists who worked with him :

In my intercourse with you I have often dimly felt the bitter and eating anxiety which was always with you, the ceaseless strain and responsibility ; have often pictured your nightly return to your office and thought how often the news then gained must have been a soul-sickening nightcap. I have felt for you in the hope deferred or crushed and all the time I have wondered — wondered at the great heart that could carry it all and have something over for others. I tell you it was often your unbounded optimism and faith in the future that many a time has lifted me up to new struggles. It was an example to all who came near you. You are the most cheery soul that ever encouraged a man — no matter how dark and nearly hopeless the way, the bright smile and loud cheery voice always made me repeat to myself my slogan and I kept on. And the U-boats are all to surrender and this has the D.A.S.D. accomplished.

CAPTAIN, H.M.S. *IRON DUKE*

ADMIRAL SIR JOHN DE ROBECK

ADMIRAL SIR JOHN DE ROBECK AND STAFF, H.M.S. *IRON DUKE*
Commodore Fisher on right of Admiral

CHAPTER VII

1919-1921

Captain, H.M.S. *Iron Duke*, Mediterranean Fleet — Russian Civil War — Difficulties with Turkey — Chief of Staff to Sir John de Robeck, Commander-in-Chief, Mediterranean

When the Armistice was signed Fisher was forty-three. The whole German Fleet was in our hands ; war with the United States was unthinkable ; the Japanese had fought with us in the war and were bound to us by treaty ; and it seemed extremely unlikely that the British Fleet would be called on for anything more important than police work in the lifetime of the existing senior officers. Fisher thought his real work in the Navy was finished and felt fully young enough to begin a new career in the field of politics. It is interesting to think what part he might have played. He had many friends in the House of Commons ; he was, for a naval officer, well versed in world affairs and he was an easy and fluent speaker.

When he was commander of the *Princess Royal*, building at Barrow-in-Furness, he became deeply interested in social questions, visited mines and factories, studied the lives of the people, and seriously considered entering politics. On that occasion his promotion to captain at a very young age diverted him from politics. Happily for the Navy, there was now no seat immediately available and he returned to naval life to find that, so far from proving an anti-climax, its greatest interest and greatest responsibilities were still to come.

On 1st February, 1919, he was appointed captain of the

Iron Duke, shortly proceeding to join the Mediterranean Fleet. It is necessary to sketch in the political background of his work during the next few years, as the situation in Eastern Europe was extremely complicated and highly charged, owing to the civil war in Russia and the delays in coming to terms with the Turks. Allied troops had occupied Odessa and other Black Sea ports after the Armistice, but the French evacuated Odessa in April, 1919. However, in the autumn, General Denikin's operations against the Bolsheviks prospered and by September he was in Kieff. The policy of the Allies was to support the anti-Bolshevik forces but, owing to war-weariness and the spread of Communism, the French were a broken reed.

By December the Bolsheviks had collected sufficient strength to counter-attack and by the summer of 1920 they had captured Denikin's last base at Novorossiisk. A later attempt by General Wrangel to recover the situation met with some success, but by November he, too, had been defeated.

The Turkish situation was even more complicated. Peace treaties had been concluded with Germany, Austria, and Bulgaria, but it was not till early in 1920 that the British, French, and Italian Governments made a serious attempt to conclude a Treaty with the Turks. The principal demands made by the Allies were that Thrace, Tenedos, and Imbros and a large area of Asia Minor, which included the important port of Smyrna, should be handed over to the Greeks ; that Syria, Armenia, the Hedjaz and Mesopotamia should be given independence, and that an International Commission appointed by the League of Nations should control the Dardanelles, Bosphorus and Sea of Marmora. The Turks reacted violently to these terms and the situation became pregnant with difficulties when two Governments appeared in Turkey — one at Angora under the leadership of Mustapha Kemal, which was prepared to resist with force any occupation by a foreign Power, and the other at Constantinople, which was prepared to come to terms with the Allies. By July, 1920, the Greeks, supported by the Allies, had occupied all the territory ceded to them and had driven back Mustapha Kemal's forces, which had not yet gathered strength. In August a treaty of peace was signed by the Allies and the Turkish Constantinople Government, but without the approval of Mustapha Kemal, who was steadily gaining adherents to the Nationalist party.

During 1921 the Nationalist strength and influence steadily increased and Mustapha Kemal informed the Powers that his was now the only Government and that his intention was to return to Constantinople. In June the Italians withdrew; in October the French began to withdraw their forces, which had been buttressing the Greeks and Armenians; the latter, fearing the wrath of Mustapha Kemal, began to pack up their household goods ready for flight.

By 1922 Kemal was the ruler of Turkey, but the Allies would not agree to his demand that the Greeks should return to their own country as a prerequisite to discussing peace terms. In September he swept the Greeks out of Smyrna and prepared to invade the neutral zone occupied by the Allied troops at Chanak on the Anatolian side of the Dardanelles. Thanks to the great tact and firmness displayed by the British delegate, General Sir Charles Harington, there was no bloodshed and an Armistice was signed on 11th October.

Fisher was overjoyed to be on the bridge of a ship again, with the blue sky overhead and the brilliant Mediterranean colours on which to feast his eyes. From Malta, where he arrived on the 1st of April, 1919, he wrote:

Wonderful weather all the way. Straits of Gibraltar at sunrise, violet and green Spanish hills. Then Gib. and clusters of houses baked in morning sun. Hot blue waters all the way here. Off the harbour at 9 A.M. Gorgeous morning. Steamed slowly up ; large crowds of Maltese on either shore. We got to our berth turning a complete circle in rather narrow waters without help of tugs. Valetta perfectly exquisite. It seems like some beautiful dream. If only you could be here too. Hot sun, but all the trees and shrubs fresh green and flower-beds brilliant and a most gorgeous claret-coloured creeper with large flowers climbing up the walls. Have never felt about Malta as I have this morning. The opera is still on, *Othello* tonight, *Manon* tomorrow ; Shall I go ? Yaas — I think so !

At Malta he heard that the Commander-in-Chief, Sir S. Gough-Calthorpe, who was also British High Commissioner at Constantinople, was in Egypt and that he would probably meet him at Crete, and, after taking him on board, go on to Alexandria if the situation in Egypt cleared up.

The Egyptian situation eased and by the 8th of April Fisher was at Constantinople, which was frequently to be his base during the next two years. He found the city of absorbing interest with its much-swollen population of Russian refugees and officers and officials of many nations ; the lovely scenery and colours of the Bosphorus and the surrounding country always stirred him deeply :

Had a good pull in the skiff with Flag Lieutenant before breakfast. This is now an established bit of routine. Up at 7 A.M. Shave. Eat an orange. In the boat at 7.30. A hard pull over to Pera till we are out of the mill race, then dawdle up close in-shore watching the maritime life of the place, loading and unloading of huge wine and oil barrels, timber, corn, cattle — past mosques and walled gardens stretching down to the water's edge with chestnut and fruit blossom, then out into the Bosphorus again and back on board about 8.10. Cold bath. Muscles hard as iron. Breakfast at 8.30, and quite ready for it.

Oh, my criky, haven't I roared over Daisy Ashford. I seem to *know* the face. Who is it — some old head put on a young body ? Not finished yet and then all the staff must read it.

Mind you read Loti's *Désenchantées* — it will give you an insight into *our* life here.

During that uneasy period British naval officers had often to use their initiative to deal with unexpected situations :

Got on board about midnight to find a large steamer making S.O.S., shouting across the water "Send help, there is mutiny." This was much better, and in a trice I was in a picket-boat with twenty marines armed to the teeth. Found a ship full of refugees and officers. Bolsheviks on board who had just held a meeting and decided to blow up the ship. I said, "Produce them." A great hunt followed. A lot of jabbering. They had all fled and hidden. At last one was caught, a plucky little chap. A big Russian Colonel accused him. I let him go on the condition that if there was any symptom of a rising or any complaint made by any Russian officer, all the suspects would be shot at once. This pleased everyone and there has been peace ever since.

It was typical of Fisher, though a senior captain, to collect a few marines and go himself to deal with the situation. "This was much better" was the glad cry of a man who would never miss the slightest chance of an adventure.

He saw clearly all the weaknesses of the policy we were pursuing at the time :

Bed at 6 A.M., reflecting what an interesting part of the world this is, but how I long for One Country, One policy, One man to carry it out. As it is, it is 5 Countries, 50 policies, 500 people all working irrespective of one another.

International chaos instead of concert about sums it up.

During April ships of the Mediterranean Fleet were employed in the Black Sea giving aid to General Denikin. The situation for the anti-Bolshevik forces was deteriorating and on the 23rd of April the Commander-in-Chief decided to go himself to the scene of operations in the *Iron Duke*.

The next week was an exciting one for Fisher, and his

diary is most interesting, as it illustrates the activities and difficulties of the Navy, committed to supporting one side in a civil war, and how, even when preoccupied with serious affairs, he still fully enjoyed the beauties of nature :

Wednesday, April 23rd, 1919.—Got news of the meeting of French ships at Sevastopol. C-in-C decided to go there. Left Constantinople at noon. Most heavenly trip up the Bosphorus. Sunshine and cloud. Brilliant greens, soft pinks, and dazzling white palaces and houses. The best thing I've ever seen. Entered Black Sea at 2 P.M.

Thursday, 10.0.—Passed Balaclava quite close. Saw the old St. George's Monastery where our soldiers used to fraternise with the Russian Monks.

11.0.—Anchored off Sevastopol. French very disaffected. Insist on going home at once. One big battleship, *La France*, already sailed. The remainder won't work. Hoisted Red Flag for a short time. Greek soldiers fired on a party of French sailors on shore. Very bad feeling. French Battleship wanted to fire on Greek Battleship. Greek ships sarcastically hoisted dummy figure of a sailor being hanged at the yardarm for Mutiny. Greeks have humour. Bolsheviks are all round the town. French have allowed a Soviet to enter. Armistice declared till policy is known. French Admiral told pretty clearly British opinion of all this.

Friday.—Landed and inspected all warlike material. Guns, mines, ammunition ships, submarines, etc. Started sinking all submarines. Disabled all Russian Battleships and Destroyers by blowing up their engines. French looking on ; Bolsheviks also looking on but not interfering.

Saturday.—Left Sevastopol at 11 A.M. for Theodosia. Passed Lividia, Emperor's summer Palace, and Yalta. Very beautiful. Anchored off Theodosia at 8 P.M. This is a Bolshevik stronghold. Searchlight on the town all night. We move off at 7.0 tomorrow to bomb Bolsheviks who are advancing against Volunteer Army between this place, Theodosia, and Kertch. If the Bolsheviks can cross from Kertch to Mainland of Caucasus they will defeat Denikin and Volunteer Army and imperil our Army in Caucasus and our ships in Caspian.

Sunday.—Moved down opposite the lines that the Volunteer

Army are holding. We got there at 8, anchored close to shore —a lovely green rolling plain with high hills in the distance and low ones above the beach. From the right came a bunch of cavalry, then another, then a long winding line of cavalry, then wheeled vehicles and more cavalry. All very spirited as if on manœuvres. *Centaur* and *Caradoc* firing at some distant Bolshevik position which I couldn't see. Then quite suddenly, as this gallant-looking Volunteer Army came riding gaily past the ship, a heavy rifle and machine gun fire was brought to bear on them from concealed trenches and a good deal of confusion resulted. Word was sent off to us that the Bolshevik Headquarters were in a village about 8 miles off, which we couldn't see, but we sent up a seaplane and laid our guns by the chart and our first shot was only 100 yards from the railway station which was an important junction. So we fired some broadsides and destroyed it. The Bolsheviks abandoned the town and fled with our faithful triends behind them.

Monday.—At Sevastopol. French and Greek troops evacuating the town as fast as they can. Bolsheviks closing in. I went in at 7 A.M. to blow up a Russian submarine and to disable two destroyers. Had great difficulty in clearing the crowds away before the explosions took place. Had a Lewis gun covering the operation. I should like to have walked further out of the town. The Russian Churches are so jolly, at Sevastopol not so much as all along the South Coast of Crimea. Most wonderful blazing bright gold domes, others sapphire blue with gold stars on them. We could have held Sevastopol with the Greeks and without the French but the French General who commands all armies on shore ordered evacuation and nothing could alter him.

Tuesday.—Left at 11.0 for Constantinople. I have already described the voyage down or up the Bosphorus. As a matter of fact it can't be described, there's nothing to approach it anyhow at this time of year. Lovely little creeks and valleys full of delicate green trees or pink blossom and here and there a terra-cotta house or village or shining white villa, and the view changing as you round each bend of the Channel opening fresh mosques and heights.

These extracts are not only interesting as a description of the activity and difficulties of the Navy at that period, but illustrate Fisher's intense love of the beauties of nature ; even when the guns are about to open fire he has time to enjoy some lovely colouring or stretch of scenery.

In May he was again involved in a difficult situation produced by the Allies' strange decision to support with armed force the Greeks who were about to land at Smyrna and occupy part of Anatolia. All Fisher's keen sense of justice rebelled against this use of British power, which eventually brought disaster to the Greeks and cost them thousands of lives. He sailed on 13th May, with the High Commissioner on board, for Smyrna. There he found an Italian Dreadnought, an American Dreadnought, and two French Dreadnoughts as well as Greek battleships and destroyers.

The Admiral at once called a conference, and it was decided that the British, French, and Italians should occupy certain ports in preparation for the Greek Army to land in Smyrna. Fisher sent 120 men on shore to man a fort and the next day the Greek transports started arriving. The Turkish population were very depressed, and the Italians very angry as they had hoped for Smyrna themselves. It was expected that the occupation would be peacefully effected, but the noise of heavy rifle-fire soon dispelled these hopes. Despite firm agreement with the Greeks about the treatment of the Turks, the Greeks had started shooting and the streets were soon running with blood. The British Admiral took immediate action, and with the support of the Greek Admiral, who took charge over the heads of the Greek Army officers, restored order. But all through the night messages were arriving which aroused fears that a general massacre of Turks was taking place in the surrounding country. Fisher, with his keen sense of justice, felt deeply about the policy that had produced this holocaust and about the disgraceful behaviour of the Greek soldiery.

The dear old Turkish Vali [he wrote] to whom we had to make known the news of Smyrna being lost to Turkey and handed over to her greatest enemy, was actually shot at by Greek soldiers, his wife hit in the leg, her watch stolen and his fez torn up by the mob. That has all been stopped now and the Vali knows he owes it to us. It was pathetic to hear the old boy talk — quite sincere he was I'm sure when he said it was heart-breaking to find England, the one Country they respected and could obey, against them and delivering them chained and bound to Greece of all Countries.

Statesmanship in Europe was at a low ebb, and the opinion of the "man on the spot", in close touch with a complex situation, was of little interest to the tired and, in some cases, ignorant old gentlemen who were remaking the map of Europe far away in the capitals.

It was not very long before the Turks, under the brilliant leadership of Mustapha Kemal, asserted themselves and bustled the Greeks out of the Smyrna district.

In August, 1919, the *Iron Duke* became the flagship of the new Commander-in-Chief, Sir John de Robeck, and he asked Fisher to serve as his Chief of Staff, with the rank of Commodore, 2nd Class.

Thus began a happy and profitable companionship between two men of outstanding character, personality, and fine presence which lasted five years. It was a very happy period for Fisher — "De Robeck is such a fizzer to go about with because the moment anyone sees him and his laugh and manners generally, they all want to help". It was a testing appointment, as de Robeck hated paper work and left much to his Chief of Staff.

This job [wrote Fisher] is like being a Doctor and a Lawyer. One writes and interviews all day. In the evening one reads reports, Naval, Military and Political, from Rome, Athens, Bulgaria, Russia, Turkey, Red Sea, Egypt, and letters of proceedings of all ships serving away from the Flag. At any and every moment come signals and telegrams which one has to answer personally, so that one is always in harness. I love it all and do it with the least possible fuss.

In January, 1920, the *Iron Duke* left Constantinople for a short stay at Malta and Fisher was overjoyed at the chance of seeing his family again. There was great excitement when he arrived :

> Saw kids on the roof of the house. Flags waving, coloured streamers flying in the wind. We came to our buoy right under the house. I landed at 12.0. Nevil in a sailor suit and silver head the first to spot me, then fat old Ros and spindly Racy, both looking so well and fresh. Little Charles, such a character, sturdy, fine full head, full of energy.

He managed to squeeze in three dances, three dinner parties, three operas, tennis, and some motor expeditions before the sudden news of a White Russian *débâcle* broke up the happy party.

When he left Constantinople he feared that Denikin would crumple up and that the Bolshevik wave would soon engulf everything, but the many telegrams and conferences had ended in nothing except that, if the worst happened, the British Navy was to give every assistance to Russians who wished to be evacuated. Before leaving for Malta, Fisher had been hard at work making skeleton plans for embarking tens of thousands of White Russians, and in the minimum time, as it was expected that the Bolsheviks would show little mercy to their opponents. The enmity between the French and Italians had eased his work as they disagreed on every point, so one could always be relied on to support any British proposal.

Now these plans had to be completed and implemented, and as quickly as possible.

> We are steaming at top speed [Fisher wrote] to endeavour to save the thousands of wounded and all the women and children from Novorossiisk from falling into the hands of the

Bolsheviks. My last 24 hours was spent in collecting hospital ships, transports, blankets, food, morphia, coal, hot bottles, etc. and I've stripped Malta. We may have to extricate 6000 wounded and 30,000 women and children, and the weather will be bitter cold — probably 30 below zero. It was hard to leave Malta but more bearable as we have a real bit of work to do.

The Allied Governments, driven hither and thither by self-interest and political currents, were certainly placing heavy responsibilities on the shoulders of British naval officers, and the Commander-in-Chief was fortunate to have Fisher with him when there was so much hard thinking to be done and so much to organise. Fisher's view immediately after the war that he might have no more useful work to do in the Navy was proving very wide of the mark.

After the liquidation of the Bolshevik question, which in its final stage of evacuating tens of thousands of unfortunate people, who had lost all their worldly goods, called for a tremendous effort by officers and men, the British Fleet enjoyed a period of comparative peace.

Fisher visited Port Said, Alexandria, Beyrout, and Haifa, seeing as much as possible of the people and the surrounding country. "Beyrout is wonderful," he wrote, "and Mt. Carmel, which I visited from Haifa, very memorable, looking on the Brook Kishon, Plain of Esdraelon and Mt. Hermon. Look up your geography and Old Testament."

That was in May 1921, and he was already prophesying that more trouble lay ahead: "Not certain which Country will be in the soup first, Syria or Palestine. The former will be attacked by the Turks, I expect, and, if so, the Arabs will probably rise against the Jews, and, exasperated by our policy, may make it uncomfortable for the English."

But the next trouble was at Constantinople, where the relations between the Allies and the Turks were steadily deteriorating, and the *Iron Duke* returned there in June. The history of the Turkish question has already been briefly outlined, but some extracts from a comprehensive review of the situation as it appeared to Fisher in September 1920 show what lay behind the conditions that now had to be faced :

> I may be wrong but the conviction has been steadily growing in my mind that the present inter-allied diplomatic procedure in Constantinople is nearing the end of its tether as regards practical usefulness. The interests of the three powers are becoming too divergent to permit of their being harnessed together much longer — for the cart to move two horses at least must pull in the same direction.
>
> . . . .
>
> Turkish Unionists are undoubtedly cordial partisans and look to the essential reconstruction of an extended Turkish Empire, following first the expulsion of all British influence, and possibly later that of Russia, their present ally.
>
> . . . .
>
> As regards the remainder of Anatolia, except for the extreme Western tip, it is still in the hands of the Nationalists and no one has yet been able to suggest suitable means of wresting the Country from their grip.
>
> Italy, with whom we are apparently walking hand in hand concerning Russia, is entirely sympathetic to Mustapha Kemal, who, in turn, in alliance with the Bolsheviks, is entirely hostile to us. Can any situation be fuller of inconsistencies ?
>
> There is much talk at the moment concerning the formation of a Greek Republic which shall gather together and protect the Greek Communities that lie between Trebizond and Erzerum. Greek aspirations do not, however, I imagine, stop there. The acquisition of Constantinople itself and further portions of Anatolia are undoubtedly at the back of their minds.
>
> Thus we have Great Britain, France and Italy all without the sinews of war and yet endeavouring to advance their own aims by means other than force. Greece alone with power and waiting to use it, waiting for the signal to go. France *with* Great Britain as regards the Kemalists, France *against*

Great Britain as regards Wrangel. Italy *with* Great Britain as regards Soviet relations. Italy *against* Great Britain as regards Kemalists. Great Britain, who a short time back was predominant and respected in South Russia, Transcaucasia, Persia, Mesopotamia, and the length and breadth of Anatolia, is today without a friend, and with scarcely any remaining prestige.

. . . .

The Italians have sought every means of damaging our cause both in these Countries and Egypt. There is no need to go further along the road hand in hand with Italy especially when the other hand holds a dagger.

Greece has undoubtedly been useful and for her services has been paid in full. It is no part of our policy to see Turkey further dismembered, and I would be opposed to any fresh advance on the part of the Greeks.

It should surely be within the power of our diplomatists to arrive at a complete understanding with France concerning the Near East, the objects we each have in view, the methods we propose to employ to effect our ends. Without such an understanding I can see little hope of escaping from the impasse now created. Our differences with France are exploited here in Anatolia you may be quite sure to the full and such differences tend to keep the situation unstable everywhere. A declaration of common policy, a statement of common action to be taken would be a knockout blow for the Kemalists, who, as ever, undertake to count on our incapacity to pull together.

But there had been no common action and now the Turks were fighting the Greeks who were trying to jump a large tract in Anatolia, and the Allied Governments very apprehensive about the future.

Having occupied Constantinople in March, 1920, the Allies were at sixes and sevens what to do next in view of the growing strength of the Kemalists. The Constantinople Turkish Government, which had no funds or credit, could not administer the city; if the French took over the administration, they would pursue a French policy opposed to the policy of the other Allies ; the only course was for us to remain strong at Constantinople, Scutari, and the towns on the eastern shores of the Bosphorus, using the Greek offensive as a lever to induce the Turks to accept the Allies' peace proposals by a promise that we would bring all possible pressure on the Greeks to halt if they did so.

The complex situation threw a heavy burden of work on Fisher, as Chief of Staff to our representative, and he was constantly occupied in disentangling intelligence reports, interviewing representatives of the other interested parties and drafting memoranda. The scope of his work can be realised from the numerous objects the British Government were hoping to achieve. We wanted to stop the Turks and Greeks fighting in Anatolia, to stop the Kemalist-Bolshevik alliance, to keep the Turks in Constantinople as the least of many evils, to keep the peace with the French and Italians, to safeguard so far as possible British lives and interests, and to make a firm Treaty with the Turks. But there were too many cooks stirring the broth and by the summer of 1921 Mustapha Kemal, now in considerable strength, was causing the Allies grave anxiety.

In July Fisher was in the thick of it again :

I've been having a nailing time lately, the great excitement being the advance of the Nationalists towards Constantinople. They got within two hours by rail, and all along the South Coast of Marmora, threatening Dardanelles and Bosphorus, and we had no serious troops to stop them.

Our seaplanes and big guns just managed to do the trick at Ismid, which was the critical point, and we have since had naval operations at various points on the coast which have been much enjoyed by the sailors. Had a splendid round-up of a town called Mudani four days ago. Arrived at dawn first streak, landed 1000 men, surrounded the place, took the principal officials prisoners and read a proclamation in Turkish. At another town the Turk was one too many for us. He had got wind we were coming and the beach was lined with armed troops and all the children bathing in front of their rifles. He sent off the Greek Bishop to say that the Turkish civil population had left some hours before — only Greeks, about 10,000, remained and all was ready to burn the town, inflammables being placed in ten different places. We were nonplussed and, what I think was wise, admitted we could not punish the guilty without hurting the innocent and therefore were withdrawing.

I can't describe the Dardanelles or Bosphorus by moonlight or early morning; I seem to have been going up and down continually in the past week and the Bosphorus certainly beats anything I've ever seen. The poor old Turk is going to get the knock pretty badly I'm afraid, but it may bring about peace all the quicker. The blame principally rests with the French and Italians. They have shown great sympathy with the Turk during the Armistice. We have never gone forward an inch though it is us they wanted, and no one else. The other Allies have been telling Mustapha all along that the English don't mean to do anything, have no resources, and that with a stiff upper lip the Peace Treaty will be modified. De Robeck in grand form and we are going to have one or two more digs on the coast, great fun blowing up all the Dardanelles forts — not one blooming gun left.

Much of Fisher's time was spent in organising naval support for the Army under Sir Charles Harington. He worked for long hours with the Army staff, elaborating every detail for all eventualities. September came, and though Kemal had stated that he did not consider himself at war with Great Britain and had suggested the two Governments might well establish political relations, the only action so far had been the presentation of a joint note by the British, French, and Italian High Commissioners warning Kemal not to infringe the Neutral Zone. The French were, all the time, hand in glove with Kemal.

The main object given to the British naval Commander-in-Chief was to prevent the passage of the

Kemalists from Asia to Europe ; General Sir Charles Harington's object was to hold with his Army, Chanak, Constantinople and the Asiatic side of the Bosphorus. The naval Commander-in-Chief also had to make plans for withdrawal of the Army if the worst happened.

This is not the place to rewrite the history of those tense days ; sufficient to say that the Allies, who were never clear what they wanted, were no match for Mustapha Kemal, who knew exactly what he wanted and was leading a united and reinvigorated people.

Fisher was not present when the Turkish crisis was eventually resolved, as his Admiral had handed over the command to Admiral Sir O. de B. Brock. He, no doubt, regretted that he did not take part in the final stages, but he had been working at high pressure ever since the Armistice and must have welcomed a change to a more peaceful life.

IN THE ROUGH

WAITING FOR THE EVENING FLIGHT

CHAPTER VIII

1922-1930

Chief of Staff, Atlantic Fleet — Rear-Admiral, Mediterranean Fleet — Director Naval Intelligence — Fourth Sea Lord — Deputy Chief of Naval Staff — Cruiser Question — 1930 London Naval Conference

SLOWLY, very slowly, despite continual quarrels amongst the so-called Allies, peace came to Europe and it was not till eleven years later that Fisher, when Commander-in-Chief Mediterranean, was again in a Fleet on a war footing. The Naval Estimates were now attuned to the Government ruling that there could be no war for ten years ; ships in commission were kept to a minimum, and oil fuel for exercises and cruises was severely limited.

It is in such periods that the British naval officer, true to the traditions of his service, is at his best. It is easy and natural to strive for high efficiency in war-time or when war threatens but, as other maritime nations have found, it is not so easy to maintain enthusiasm when it is most unlikely that the guns will ever be fired in earnest and probable that the ships themselves will come to the age for scrapping before required for any serious business. Yet, during those years between the termination of the First World War and the first movements on the Continent that awoke the sleepy, peaceful world to the grim fact that the Treaty of Versailles had only brought temporary respite and that the League Covenant was a broken reed, the officers and men of the Navy never relaxed. There was just the same keenness as ever to obtain a high performance at the various firings, just the same high endeavour to win the regatta or the Marathon, just the same eagerness to be the cleanest and smartest ship in the Fleet, and at the same time unremitting effort to keep abreast of the times and develop the new Anti-Aircraft gunnery and the Fleet Air Arm, which was rapidly gaining in importance.

Fisher, as Chief of Staff to Sir John de Robeck for three years in the Mediterranean Fleet and afterwards for two years in the Atlantic Fleet, played a considerable part in keeping up the high standard. Whatever he did, he did with all his might, and as Chief of Staff he was in a position to make his influence felt in every activity of the Fleet. His enthusiasm sometimes evoked criticism from the captains when signals were made to them in the name of the Commander-in-Chief calling attention to some fault in the appearance of their ship or boats at a time when they knew the Commander-in-Chief was away. It is an unwritten law of the Navy that praise or blame must only come from the Commander-in-Chief in person and never from the staff using his name.

But their resentment was short-lived, as no one could fail to appreciate Fisher's single-minded devotion to his chief, who would not tolerate any falling-off from a standard that had endured for a hundred years.

Those years with de Robeck were some of the happiest of his life. He had the greatest admiration for his tall, distinguished-looking chief; the two formed a rare combination of talents. British interests had been very safe in their hands during critical times in the Near East and the Fleet had prospered exceedingly and maintained its traditional efficiency under their rule.

Fisher was very upset when some criticisms of de Robeck appeared in a book. He was burning to write to *The Times* but Lord Jellicoe, who had consulted the First Lord, dissuaded him, as he was at the time on full pay. The last paragraph of the unpublished letter was this :

As Chief of Staff to Sir John for five years immediately following the war when he was High Commissioner, Constantinople, Commander-in-Chief of the Mediterranean and subsequently Atlantic Fleet, I feel competent to say that in the Navy the honour and reputation of Sir John is in very safe keeping. The grandeur of the man, who inspired implicit trust and devotion in all whom he commanded, can no more be shaken by " Memoirs " than the Rock of Gibraltar by the treacherous Levanter.

Fisher was promoted to Rear-Admiral on 1st November, 1922, and continued as Chief of Staff in that rank.

In September, 1924, he was appointed Rear-Admiral of the First Battle Squadron and once more returned to the Mediterranean. This was always a first appointment for a Rear-Admiral and was for one year.

Fisher had served in battleships ever since he left the *Hawke* as a young lieutenant and it is probable that he hoped for a cruiser squadron so as to enlarge his experience, but the seagoing Fleet was much reduced at that period and there were very few appointments for junior flag officers.

He hoisted his flag in the *Barham* and, though the next year was comparatively uneventful, he was very happy cruising in waters now so familiar, but which never lost their charm for him. From Milo he wrote :

Sea like a satin sheet. Enclosed harbour. Exquisite sunrise. Ship hardly made a ripple as she glided in. Sugar-loaf hills, very bare and hot-looking with dazzling white villages perched about that in the distance look like snow, not unlike Malta but much more irregular, and heather and scrub over the sides of the hills.

Have just come off after a good evening tramp. The sun turned everything to gold and purple and I took my gun on the chance of meeting a quail or partridge but saw none. Stood by a lake as the moon got up and saw some duck wheeling very high but they never came down, but to stand there and see the reflections on the hills and feel the enveloping stillness was enchanting. Am going to pull ashore in the skiff at 6 A.M. tomorrow to enjoy the early morning scents and to bathe in a sandy cove.

And from Volo :

Had a jolly walk solo this evening. New moon challenging crimson sunset. Graceful peasants plodding home after their work. Tranquillity and fragrance everywhere.

He was delighted when the *Barham* won the regatta, and with her all-round efficiency ; and when she sailed for England in September, he wrote that he " missed her awfully ", though his own time was almost up and he only flew his flag in the *Valiant* for four weeks.

The Commander-in-Chief, Sir Roger Keyes, visited the ship a day or two before she left the Fleet :

He went round all the men and then we marched past and then he stayed to Church. Then he made a farewell speech. Now the march past was the most moving thing I've ever seen. I had to keep a frozen jaw to prevent dissolving. And R. K. was the same. It was something quite inexplicable. Officers and men looked so magnificent that the lumps would rise in the throat. And when R. K. had all hands up to say farewell he could scarcely speak. I liked him for that. He said the *Barham* was a Man-of-War in the completest sense of the word, happy, smart, efficient — and how he felt her loss, how sorry he was to think that her present Captain would no longer be in command when she came out again, and to my astonishment he then turned round and said " and I'm sure you have felt proud to fly the flag of the Rear-Admiral for whom I predict a brilliant future ! " Of course he didn't mean that — but he was so carried away by the whole business that he was prepared to say anything ! I did like him for being able to see into the minds of the men.

It was a very great morning.

There followed ten months on half-pay, and though, with his vigorous mind, he cannot have welcomed a period of unemployment, there was the compensation that he was able at last to be with his family.

He was a most devoted father and always demanded every detail about his children when away from them. He had every reason to be proud of them, as they were blessed with good looks and were very intelligent.

The country was passing through one of those oft-repeated periods in its history when, lulled by the words of great promise in the preamble to the last treaty — " There shall be a universal and perpetual peace " — the strength of the Defence Forces attracted little interest.

It was now over 150 years since Lord Hawke had worn himself out in his endeavours to convince the Government of the day that the Seven Years' War was not the last war and that, unless a nucleus of ships was kept in commission and money provided for a steady building programme, the Fleet would not be ready when the next inevitable quarrel arose with the French ; and after every major war since those days Hawke's successors had had to fight hard to prevent the Navy being starved and its strength so reduced that it would not be able to perform its functions if war broke out. Parsimony over expenditure on the Navy was serious enough in the days of the wooden walls, but it is far more serious now that steel ships with their complicated mechanisms have taken their place, because they are quite unfit to fight unless every officer and man is highly trained ; and training is a matter of years, not weeks.

Fisher, who had always devoted much thought to major strategy and the conduct of a future war, was disturbed at the apathy about our naval needs, and whilst on half pay wrote an article for the *National Review* which he called " The Sea, the Air, and the Nation ".

When he wrote the dive-bomber had not yet appeared, nor was the destructive power of the bomb and torpedo so great as it is today. His anticipation that the Fleet operating within an enemy air zone would always have what is now termed " an air umbrella " has unfortunately not come true. But the article is a clearly-reasoned statement of the respective rôles of the Navy and the Air Force in war and is as true today as when it was written — thirteen years before the outbreak of the Second World War — and some extracts are, therefore, of interest :

There are those who will point out that the situation has undergone considerable change since 1914. There is the Washington Agreement, which is regarded as the first step — and a very important one — to some general scheme of disarmament, and there is the newly realized potentiality of the Air Force.

. . . . . .

The achievements of the Air Force and the advances it may confidently be expected to make in the future are, however, matters very much bound up with those of the Navy. It is commonly said that Great Britain is no longer an island, and recently that we suffer under a positive disability through being surrounded by the sea. Though the conquest of the air has provided an alternative means of travel, aircraft can never, by any stretch of imagination, replace shipping for the conveyance of armies and the revictualling of a country such as ours.

If the British Navy holds the surrounding seas, invasion on any scale to be worth undertaking is just as impossible today as it was throughout the Great War.

It would not be extravagant to imagine an army of, say, 10,000 men, escorted by a sufficiency of fighting planes, making a descent on some part of England. They would be troublesome, but confronted by troops with every military resource at hand, the principal of which would be that of unlimited ammunition, they could not be expected to maintain themselves for long, to say nothing of the attacks from our own Air Force, which, though it may have been unable to materially hinder the passage of the enemy air army, will pay effective attention to it when it reaches the ground.

Enemy airmen may inflict great damage or loss on us by bombing crowded centres and gassing wide areas. They will undoubtedly attack dockyards, shipping, wharves, railway stations, power stations, fuel stores, and food depots.

All these things, hitherto inviolate by virtue of the sea, can now be reached. But the answer is not that the Navy has ceased to be any protection, but to that particular threat we must look to the air and land forces (*e.g.* high-angle guns, searchlights, range-finders, and sound-locators), whilst the Navy interposes a barrier against invasion on any scale which could force the country to surrender. Dislocation and suffering we must expect, but we are still only at the beginning as regards the devising of methods of protection of critical areas from aerial attack. There is only one answer to the question, " What is the use of a Navy when an enemy can paralyse the life of a nation by a series of air attacks directed at its heart ? " and that is, that it is no use.

It is necessary to take special measures to protect the heart. It is not far short of the truth to say that it is for the air and land forces to protect the heart whilst the Navy feeds the body. Death may ensue by either stab or starvation.

Can it be said that the Navy can insure against the latter ? First of all, is the Fleet itself proof against modern air attack ? There are a good many reasons that prompt a confident answer. Firstly, that it is not generally or even usually necessary for the Fleet to exercise its protective or blockading functions within the radius of action of shore-based enemy aircraft. Secondly, that if the Fleet is compelled to act within an enemy air zone it will be accompanied by its fleet air arm — squadrons in the aircraft carriers reinforced by fighters from individual ships. Those who have watched the progress of this new arm of the Navy have little fear as to its ability to maintain a patrol that will give warning of the approach of danger and deal faithfully with the enemy craft when they arrive. Thirdly, to make a successful attack on a ship moving at high speed with either a bomb or torpedo the plane must come close or low. The great advance made in high-angle fire and its control renders either an operation of great danger, whilst the disposition of destroyers or other light craft round the capital ships, which ensures a warm reception for torpedo planes at the very points they would select for firing, is an added deterrent. Fourthly, our ships are now built especially to withstand the bomb and torpedo.

Can enemy air power prevent our shipping reaching port in spite of a watchful Fleet in being?

The Bristol Channel, Southampton, the Thames, the Humber, and the Tyne will probably lie within the zone of Continental aircraft. Unquestionably those districts must have their own coastal air defence, which will provide aerial convoy to important ships on the first and last stages of their voyage as well as protect the port itself.

Other expedients will, however, be necessary. Ships must expect to have their routes altered by wireless to guide them clear of areas in which we have no air supremacy; they will have to make the best use of certain hours and non-flying weather, and, in addition to carrying anti-aircraft guns (as they did anti-submarine guns in the last war), they may have to be escorted by ships carrying aircraft themselves. In the main, however, their safety will best be assured by our shore squadrons intercepting enemy flights between their aerodromes and the focal points of our trade routes.

From enemy surface or submarine attack in home waters, and from all forms of attack in distant seas, the Navy must, as hitherto, be the protector of our merchant shipping.

The scope of such a responsibility will be realised at once if trade statistics are studied. Broadly it may be assumed that at any given moment there are not far short of a thousand large British ships actually at sea or about to sail in the Atlantic, about a third of that number in the Red Sea and the Indian Ocean, and a quarter in the Pacific.

But over and above such widespread responsibility rests the obligation of neutralising or defeating the enemy fleet and arresting all enemy sea-borne trade. It is to be hoped that the Fleet air arm will so expand as to enable the otherwise totally inadequate number of cruisers on foreign stations to discharge their duties by extending their radius of surveillance, but in any case this vast system of patrol and protection must fall entirely on the Royal Navy. The problem in its broad outlines has now been stated. It is for the Admiralty and the Air Ministry to say what provision must be made to ensure the national safety. How can such representations be rejected? Only on the score that the case has not been fairly put or that we are prepared to deliberately shut our eyes and take the risk that there will be no more war.

To say that we cannot afford to safeguard our national existence is to utter an untruth. Our expenditure on other services — mainly social — has only to be glanced at. In the present Board of Admiralty we have what we have never had before, and that which no other nation has the good fortune to possess — a body of admirals with unrivalled experience of war at sea; their credentials are of the highest, though that has not spared them from the sneers of a certain class of newspaper and a certain class of politician. They have submitted with admirable patience and courtesy to the inquisitions of "business men", and though no doubt the reflection that as a Board of Directors controlling a hard-working, happy, and efficient Service they may have little to learn from any City man may have never crossed their minds, they may be forgiven for remembering that there is not a merchant sitting in his office who does not owe all he has to the seamen of today and to generations of seamen long passed away.

And yet in spite of the teaching of history and the lessons of the late war, we have the spectacle of the Sea Lords literally fighting for the bare minima of what they consider essential for the Empire's safety.

It is for our people, whose history is the history of its seamen, to spare them such struggles. It is for us to affirm once more that we live by the sea and that our destiny and salvation are indissolubly bound up with our strength at sea, and to declare that the requirements of the Fleet are not matters of Party politics or political opportunism. The needs of the Navy are, or should be, matters of the deepest concern to every man or woman in the country, for if not founded on national security, on what do all those schemes for the benefit of our people rest?

The "credo" of responsible statesmen of whatever Party should surely embrace the following tenets. That the British Empire — held together by sentiment though it may be — is not content to rely for its existence on the complaisance of any Nation or Group of Nations, and if threatened will be found to be wanting neither in the ancient virility of its people nor in the completest and most modern equipment of war.

That the provision of means to safeguard this Empire by land, sea, and air should be a first charge on the Nation's resources.

That, as in the past war, so in the future the manhood of the whole nation will be tested, and therefore the military virtues must not suffer from neglect.

The intrepidity of the airman, the stoic courage of the soldier, the undefeated resource of the sailor — these must emerge again, however long the period of peace ; and this can only be ensured if the primary duty of every citizen to defend his country is proclaimed and inculcated throughout the land.

In such a faith there is no hint of aggression — only the resolve to stand by our countrymen and fellow-subjects whatever may befall, and to suffer none to lay hands on that which they have built up — a resolve which really lies in the heart of every Briton.

And so, may it be hoped, when questions of Imperial Defence and the cost involved are debated, our Parliament may not be found wanting in vision and courage — vision to see our place in the world and the mission of our countrymen.

The late Professor Cramb described that mission as well as any : " To give all men within our Empire an English mind. To give to all men who come within its sway the mind to look at the things of man's life, at the past, at the future, from the standpoint of an Englishman. To diffuse that high tolerance in religion which has marked this Empire from its foundation . . . that love of free institutions, that pursuit of an ever higher justice and a larger freedom which rightly or wrongly we associate with the temper and character of our race, wherever it is dominant and secure. This is the conception of Empire and of England which persists through the changing fortunes of parties and the rise and fall of Cabinets. It outlives the generations. Like an immortal energy it links age to age. This undying spirit is the true England, the true Britain for which men strive and suffer in every zone and every era, which silently controls their actions and shapes their character like an inward fate — ' England '."

But this England can only be preserved by some sacrifice in peace and complete sacrifice in war.

In August, 1926, he took over the duties of Director

of Naval Intelligence from Rear-Admiral Hotham, during the latter's illness, and in April, 1927, joined the Board of Admiralty as Fourth Sea Lord.

Severe economy in armaments was still the policy, and though Fisher welcomed the opportunity of gaining an insight into the business of supplies, stores, pay, and uniforms, the work was not really to his taste. He was delighted when he was offered the appointment of Deputy Chief of the Naval Staff in April, 1928. He was now a Vice-Admiral, having been promoted in January.

> This new job [he wrote] is the only one, barring First Sea Lord, that is really worth having. I've always coveted it but never dreamt I could get it for another three years after I had been to sea again. The nature of the work is of course staff work — Policy, War Plans, Size of the Fleet, Preparation for War, Operations, Movements, Protection of Trade, Intelligence, Air, etc., and if anyone is required at Geneva it is the Deputy Chief who goes. Shall have lots to do with Cabinet and Foreign Office.

He would have been in his element if it had been a period of expansion or if there had been any threat of war, but the country had been lulled into a state of apathy about the state of its defence and still believed that the League would settle peacefully all international quarrels. Fisher took office when the Government was determined to cut down expense on the Navy, and held an influential position on the Board when the cruiser-building controversy was at its height. This is not the place to discuss that complex question. It will be sufficient to give a brief outline. In 1925 a firm policy of shipbuilding, based entirely on the needs of the Fleet in regard to the replacement of vessels which had become obsolete or were nearing their age limits, was adopted by the Government of the day. If replacements are not made the strength of the Fleet automatically declines, since nothing can stop ships wearing out. Being gradual and protracted, the process does not attract the same attention as a reduction of fleets by international agreement, but it operates none the less surely.

The laid-down programme was for three cruisers to be built each year, but in 1927 this was reduced to one ship and, in 1928, the construction of two ships that had been ordered was stopped.

By 1930 the construction of cruisers was proceeding at a rate of less than one a year and the Navy was six ships short of the modest total fixed as the minimum for security in 1925.

The exchanges between the Board and the Cabinet during this difficult period are in State papers that have not been published; and the Admiralty dockets which would reveal Fisher's part in the controversy are also not for publication.

He must have been alarmed, and we can be sure that he used all his powers of persuasion to remedy the deteriorating situation. No one could write a better minute or marshal arguments more convincingly, and it is a matter of regret that his work on the cruiser question must remain unknown.

Feeling ran high at the time and some senior officers thought that the Board should resign in protest. It was felt that they had such a good case that the Government would surrender, or that, as happened at an earlier period, the country would insist on more provision for the Navy when they realised the disquieting facts. But the resignation of a Board of Admiralty is only effective when the people sense danger. In the years between 1918 and 1930 they saw no threat to their peaceful life. They had once taken up the cry, "We want eight, we won't wait" when every schoolboy could see that a clash with Germany was inevitable sooner or later, but now there was nothing to arouse their fears or their interest in the strength of the Fleet. The resignation of the Board would have been a nine-days wonder, or of shorter duration if it had coincided with the Cup Final or a thrilling murder trial.

With his high sense of duty and sensitive nature this must have been a period of much heart-searching and anxiety for Fisher. Resignation, if all else failed, was in his mind at one period when he wrote to the Secretary of the Admiralty :

I do not anticipate trouble but would like to be clear as to the Constitutional aspect in certain eventualities.

For example, let us suppose that a Board of Admiralty puts forward a certain programme of new construction which is considered the MINIMUM appropriate at that moment.

Let us suppose that the Cabinet politely rejects it or reduces it till it is but a shadow of its former self.

The Board protests.

The Cabinet replies, "We note your protest and sympathise with it. We will even publish it. It will remain on Cabinet records. *Ours* is the responsibility. *We* take it. We are prepared to face the risk, to bear the blame if we have imperilled security."

In fact, let us suppose that the Board of Admiralty is confronted with an attitude and formula that Lord Beatty accepted from the present Prime Minister — our Singapore Strategy. Some assert that the Cabinet is the supreme executive — that all Government Departments must submit to their orders — that the B. of A. is never entitled to take or threaten to take coercive action such as resignation, which dislocates the machinery of an important Government Department, but I have doubt as to the validity of the view because :

(1) I believe the Admiralty Patent confers a definite responsibility on us that we cannot delegate even to a Cabinet.
(2) If that view were correct, a Government, which is, after all, only a temporary executive might do immense harm, the effect of which might only become apparent long after that Government had ceased office and which the permanent Admiralty would have to redress.

It is true that the resignation of the Board *may* not — and in these times one might say definitely would not — achieve the end in view, *e.g.* the acceptance of the particular measure by the Cabinet — but at least they would have registered their views and made their protest in the most effective way and at considerable personal sacrifice and thus have forced the attention of the public to an issue which, if covered by a short formula that the B. of A. disagree but the Cabinet takes the risk, could never attract attention.

There is the further point that if Admiralty advice is departed from in a marked degree (not only just 2 or 3 submarines and a sloop of new construction) the prestige of the Board demands that other advisers be sought rather than that it should continue in office executing a programme that it believes to be inadequate and indefensible. I fear unless we keep our eyes very wide open we may be suddenly confronted with a proposal that looks so innocent and is really so dangerous.

We ought to know exactly where we are.

The reply was to the effect that traditionally the corporate responsibility of the Board has always been emphasised and that, though theoretically the Board of Admiralty may resign, this is unlikely so far as all its Members are concerned, as those who are Members of the Government will probably not resign because they personally accept the Cabinet views.

But it went on to say that if the Board cannot accept the responsibility with the ships or moneys decided by the Cabinet it must theoretically say so and give way to others who will.

When, however, the matter was at last settled, Fisher did not take a gloomy view :

Last October our tonnage built was 298,000 ; we did not feel that in those days it was practical politics to ask for more than 3 cruisers a year for new construction. We were unable to wring even these out of a Conservative Government. 50 ships built therefore appeared to be all we could *hope to get*, and at the same time the absolute minimum that we *could accept*. This number at first sight looks inadequate when compared with 60 plus 10 average that used to be our guide.

But the 50 built means 59 built and building, and if there is danger there will be 3 just falling in that need not be scrapped. If we carry through the entire convention as we have drafted we shall also be able to use 10 per cent of destroyer tonnage (or 20,000 tons) for cruisers, which would give us 53 built, 9 building, 3 about to be scrapped. I hope the Service will not think that we have let them down. My honest opinion is that the number of ships and the tonnage just about represent the *maximum we could hope to get* and the *minimum we ought to have*. And the whole position is to be reviewed in 1935, when if we feel unsafe we can increase — if we feel safer we can reduce.

The 1930 London Naval Conference also took place whilst he was Deputy Chief of the Naval Staff and this threw a heavy burden of work on him, as it was the Admiralty Divisions under his direction that had to do all the spade-work and produce carefully considered arguments on the many questions that were debated before agreement was reached. At that Conference, Great Britain, the United States, Italy, and France agreed to radical alterations to the Washington Treaty. Replacement of capital ships was deferred, total tonnage of different types of ships was settled, certain ships were placed on the scrapping list, the term " aircraft carriers " was re-defined, and their tonnage and armament limited, the tonnage and armament of submarines was limited, and the contracting parties were bound to communicate to each of the other parties all details of ships laid down within a month of the laying of the keel.

Fisher himself described the treaty as " not at all bad ".

He was pleased that, with the exception of the earlier scrapping of the *Iron Duke* and *Tiger* than was agreed in the Washington Treaty, we retained our capital ships. He welcomed the agreement to limit the number of

8″ cruisers, as they were the greatest danger to our sea communications and ruinous for us to build to the requisite number if other Powers built them in numbers.

He was also pleased that the total number of cruisers did not appear in the treaty and only the total tonnage, so that we could if we wished build smaller cruisers and increase our numbers. He considered the tonnage figures for destroyers and submarines satisfactory.

He was satisfied that he had done everything possible for the Navy and letters from naval officers who realised this were a source of great pleasure to him. His old friend, Pound, wrote :

> I have not written to you before because I wanted thoroughly to digest the Naval Treaty before writing to you.
>
> Even though I know all the difficulties you have been through and how desperately hard you personally would have fought to keep our end up, I do not think I could have written had I felt that the Board had let the Service and the Country down. Having thoroughly digested it, I must say I most whole-heartedly congratulate you on having got us through so amazingly well.
>
> It was disquieting to learn that the number of cruisers had been dropped from 70 to 50, but one does realise that with the building programme having been emasculated for some years there was no chance of getting 70 before 1931. You will not acknowledge it of course, but everyone realises that you were the strong man of the party and I should like to know, but will never know, how many times you saved us from disaster.

Though it meant partial separation from his family again, Fisher must have welcomed the opportunity of going back to the blue skies and the open sea and straightforward endeavour when, in the summer of 1930, the First Lord offered him the appointment of Vice-Admiral, 2nd in Command, Mediterranean Fleet.

VICE-ADMIRAL, 2ND IN COMMAND, MEDITERRANEAN

EMBARKING IN BARGE, MALTA

CHAPTER IX

1930-1932

Vice-Admiral, 2nd in Command, Mediterranean Fleet — Night Fighting — Views on maintaining Morale

FISHER joined his new flagship, the *Revenge*, at Marseilles in October 1930.

Admiral Sir Ernle Chatfield, the Commander-in-Chief, was an officer whom he found it a delight to work under, as their views on the administration and training of the Fleet were entirely in harmony.

The long years of peace and the severe competition for promotion had affected values in the Navy. In his book *The Navy and Defence* Lord Chatfield described how he found staff work run mad and a Germanic method of preparation and organisation in existence when he took over command of the Fleet.

> I could not train the Fleet in this way [he writes]. Admirals and Captains must be ready for orders by signal by day or night, ever vigilant and ready and able instantly to make up their minds how to obey a signal in the shortest and most rapid way consistent with safety.

This was exactly Fisher's conception of the right way to train a fleet. Commanders had at one time made or marred their reputation on the performance of their ship at coaling and evolutions, and the gunnery lieutenants had earned early promotion by their ship's performance at the gunlayers' test, and this was rightly so, as the better the leadership the better the results. Now there was nothing that quite filled the place of those periodical strenuous efforts by the whole ship's company, and there was a growing tendency to attach virtue to assiduous attention to duty rather than to the attainment of results. This tendency was sometimes exaggerated into ascribing merit to an officer who never went on shore, or one who sat for long hours at his desk.

Fisher had always striven for results, and had no patience with this narrow outlook. He demanded that his ships should be supremely efficient at armament practices, spotlessly clean, well-disciplined, take a keen part in all forms of recreation, but he would have thought little of an officer who pleaded that he had never left his ship, when asked to explain a poor performance. He would have told him that if he let the other officers do more and he, himself, broadened his outlook by going ashore more frequently, the ship would be in a better state.

Though the war clouds were not yet appearing on the horizon, there were many new problems arising owing to the rapidly increasing performance of aircraft and the new conception of night fighting. Both the Commanders-in-Chief of the Atlantic and the Mediterranean Fleets were seized with the importance of training the Fleet for night fighting and thus developing a form of tactics of immense value, which would prevent an enemy escaping as they did at Jutland. Until a few years earlier all navies had accepted the difficulties of night fighting between the larger units as insurmountable. In his Jutland despatch Lord Jellicoe wrote :

> I rejected at once the idea of a night action between the heavy ships, as leading to possible disaster owing, first, to the presence of torpedo craft in such large numbers, and, secondly, to the impossibility of distinguishing between our own and enemy vessels. Further, the results of a night action under modern conditions must always be very largely a matter of pure chance.

The Official Historian of the War at Sea, too, enlarged on the theme :

> The sun had set nearly an hour before ; the gloom all round was dispersing into darkness, and any further attempt to engage must involve a night action. This, like Lord Howe on the same day in 1794, he was determined not to hazard. Modern developments had only hardened the long-established objections which condemned fleet actions by night as inadvisable.

Now difficulties which had appeared insuperable were tackled and overcome.

Fisher's resourceful and original mind was of great assistance to the Commander-in-Chief, who, after two years, was able to say that it would never again be possible for an enemy fleet to escape destruction under cover of darkness, and that night fighting would be our great opportunity in another war. These were prophetic words, for, before many years had passed, Sir Andrew Cunningham found at night, and destroyed in a few minutes, an Italian squadron of cruisers.

Fisher also bent his mind to the problem of increasing the efficiency of the anti-aircraft guns and took a leading part in many exercises to establish the best cruising formations to meet air attack and the best method of anchoring a fleet in harbour and controlling its gun-fire when air attack was expected.

Lord Chatfield has left on record the value he placed on Fisher's work :

> Fisher had left his mark on the Battle Squadron in many ways ; both in fighting efficiency and in smartness of appearance and discipline he had done much to maintain the high standard expected in the Mediterranean Fleet. No Commander-in-Chief could have hoped for a more loyal supporter. Together we did something to evolve new tactical methods and to study the problem of war in the Mediterranean against whomsoever and in whatever form it might come. I gave

him every chance to train himself for a command he would hold, and hold brilliantly. The second-in-command was in charge of the detailed administration and training exercises of the Battle Fleet, and he was responsible for much administrative work, including education of personnel. Like his brother, the historian, he was greatly interested in educational affairs. Seldom did a forenoon pass without his coming to my office to consult me about some exercise he proposed to carry out or some plan he had in mind. I think I can say we had a valuable and effective partnership for eighteen months.

Invaluable would better express the achievements of these two clear-thinking masters of their profession.

Fisher also saw eye-to-eye with Chatfield on the importance of rousing and maintaining the interest of junior officers in tactics and strategy, and of making use of their brains to further the solution of problems. Strange as it may seem, there were still senior officers serving who clung to the worn-out doctrine that tactics and strategy concerned flag officers and flag officers only, and who would allow no open discussion about exercises that had been carried out. As a result, tens of thousands of pounds were spent on oil fuel and the younger officers, the commanders in the next war, were none the wiser. One of the strange reasons given for refusing to hear the views and constructive proposals of the junior officers was that discussion without criticism was impossible, and that criticism was bad for discipline. What was bad for discipline was that junior officers thought their senior officer was not certain of himself and so was unwilling to face their questions. There was no uncertainty about Fisher. He had a flair for controlling a debate and summing-up; he never failed to collect as many officers as possible after an exercise and draw from the captains of destroyers and cruisers their experiences and views on the lessons learned. He also assembled all the officers and men concerned after an important firing and "took the chair" for a discussion after the gunnery lieutenant had completed the narrative. His method on these occasions is well illustrated by the following account, written by an officer who was at the time a junior officer of the *Revenge* :

No one who was present at the first of these meetings will ever forget the speech with which Admiral Fisher opened the proceedings. At that time there were often junior officers with only a superficial knowledge of the machinery in their charge, who felt that their rôle was to stand helplessly in the look-out position of the turret, where they could not influence in any useful way the internal organisation or the mistakes in drill, for which nevertheless they would be called to account afterwards. He first made the officers of the Turrets stand up. He pointed out that they were, each one of them, in sole and supreme charge of two 15″ guns, the most mighty weapons of their day, that there were only sixty-four 15″ guns in the Royal Navy and that their command consisted of one thirty-second part of Britain's might. It is the 15″ gun alone, he said, which is the sole bulwark of civilisation against the destructive force of Communism and it is the sole weapon upon which England and consequently the World relies for security. He then made the Gunlayers stand up and addressed them in a similar language, referring to each of them as the guardian of one-sixty-fourth part of Britain's might. This sounds like exaggerated language and grandiloquent sentiments that will hardly bear examination, but the effect at the time was magnificent. For the remainder of the commission, the officers and gunlayers went about their duties with a fresh pride. One thing is quite certain — no one except Admiral Fisher could have put across a speech of that sort and perhaps no one except Admiral Fisher would have realised that it was just what was required at that particular juncture.

That is a perfect tribute to his remarkable leadership. Just the right words used at exactly the right moment.

Fisher's day began early and, like the great Lord St. Vincent, he was always on deck at 8 A.M. to see the colours hoisted. He was quite fearless and had a predilection for performing difficult manœuvres with his ships :

The Captains of the ships were a bit surprised when I made them keep station 100 yards apart when the usual and regulation distance is 400. But they were proud as Punch when they found they could do it.

A description of Fisher at this period, written by a senior officer who was in close touch with him, is of interest as it reveals new facets of his many-sided character:

During his period in *Revenge* he visited the French Riviera, and the impression which his remarkable presence and manner produced upon the French was very marked. He was possessed of remarkable powers of insight and always saw the grotesque side of any situation. Few people could have been more indifferent to money and it would be hard to accompany anyone who made it more difficult for his companions to pay their share. It was almost a policy with him to defer the giving of praise. Silence usually followed any successful effort for long enough to make those who did not know him surprised that he had ignored it. Nevertheless the episode had been registered, and he made his comments on it generously. In this way, his approval gained an enhanced value. His life had obviously been deeply affected by the happiness of his family surroundings and he had caught, to a marked degree, the outlook of the younger generation. Unfairness invariably irritated him and he told me on more than one occasion he had removed people forcibly from queues which they had unjustifiably "cut in". His acts of kindness were unusual; at one of his parties, a woman behaved stupidly and so concerned was he that on reflection she would be upset, that he went out of his way to call on her the following day. His presence was so commanding that he naturally took charge of any situation in which he found himself, and I have seen him putting as much vigour and interest into handing out pennies to small Maltese children, as to much greater activities. Indeed, that picture is one which comes to my mind more often than any other — Sir William surrounded by half a dozen children to none of whom would he give anything until they had fallen in and taken up the positions in which he wished them to stand.

Well as Fisher now knew the towns and countries

on the Mediterranean seaboard, he always found fresh interests and new fields to explore whenever the ship anchored.

He was a voracious and discriminating reader; he was well versed in world affairs; he had kept up his classics; he enjoyed meeting interesting people, and so he never had a dull moment from the time he landed till he re-embarked.

Ships often anchored in secluded bays or off sparsely inhabited country after exercise periods or after a strenuous visit to a foreign city and there was nothing Fisher enjoyed more than organising shooting parties and including a large number of the younger officers. The latter would thoroughly appreciate the day out, but few would see all that Fisher saw and appreciated.

From a little harbour called Plateali, West Greece, he wrote:

We have cleared a bit of ground for the sailors to play football and most days we go out with our guns after duck, snipe, or woodcock. The weather is divine, no other word for it. Cold fresh nights. Hot sunny days. Wonderful sunrises and sunsets. Low hills with scattered oak trees, high mountains at the back, snow-capped, yellow reedy marshes with heat quivering above them, duck wheeling in the air. Shepherds on the hills with flocks of goats, sheep and jolly little porkers all with musical bells round their necks so that the sound, near or far, is always heard. I have seen a lot of kingfishers, a tortoise a foot across and yesterday got close to four pelicans on the water, which flapped slowly and easily away with immense wings. We are going out after duck this afternoon. All the midshipmen and some of the lieutenants are spreading across a huge marsh many miles wide.

There were also many happy days at Malta, which his boys could reach easily for their holidays; where friends came to stay; where there was the Opera, and tennis and bathing and many things dear to Fisher's heart.

It was whilst he was Second in Command that the

world was struck dumb by the news of a mutiny in the British Fleet at Invergordon. It was a terrible blow to a man of his character and unbounded pride in his service. The men of the Mediterranean Fleet stood firm and Fisher issued this finely-worded memorandum :

> Of the serious happenings in certain ships of the Atlantic Fleet recently you are all aware and I am confident that as regards them we all think alike. I say this because the heavy sacrifices demanded, in the first instance, of certain sections of the Fleet were received by you in a spirit of absolute loyalty, and representations, fully justified, were put forward in a manner no less compelling because properly made through your own officers. I did not expect otherwise from you, but nevertheless that is no reason why I should not pay my tribute to steadfastness at a moment when it was of priceless value and an example to the whole Country.
>
> In the eyes of our own people the Navy has always stood not only as a protection from all danger — a " sure shield " as the King himself has said — but also as the embodiment of all that is best in our race, courage, self-sacrifice, and devotion to duty. You have remembered this, others have forgotten it — you have not been led away, you have not provoked the contempt of foreign Countries, others have. We have to share in the general discredit and loss of trust occasioned by their conduct. You will be as anxious as I am to see our Service restored to the high place it has deservedly held in the estimation of our own people and to prove that their confidence in us, so severely shaken, can be renewed.
>
> Given an emergency such as war, the proof would be immediately forthcoming. There is nothing that could be asked of us that we would not give to the uttermost. In time of peace we can only answer by faithful service, and in the present National Crisis the Fleet can by dignity and unswerving steadiness, such as you have shown, still play a great part and redeem its good name.

He then wrote an exhaustive paper in which he analysed the causes and proposed various remedies. The facts in his view indicated the necessity of —

(*a*) Re-establishment of trust in the sympathy, justice, and, above all, the power of the Board of Admiralty.
(*b*) Greater confidence in and closer touch with their officers on the part of the lower deck.
(*c*) Raising the whole tone and morale of the men so as to be proof against subversive doctrine.

As to (*b*) he considered there was much in favour of the Army regimental system, by which officers and men were together throughout their service. Contacts between captains and officers in the Navy were so transient that the superior might hesitate to deal with the inefficient man. The naval officer said, " I expect he will be all right in some other ship " ; the regiment said, " He is ours for all time, we must make him or break him."

The Army system, however, was unworkable in the Navy, but some approach could be made to it, and he suggested reorganising the personnel into 15 divisions of about 6000 officers and men each, four at Chatham, six at Portsmouth, and five at Plymouth. His basic idea was that every cadet, boy, stoker, artisan, on joining the Active Fleet, should be posted to a division and remain in it all his time except when seconded for special service. Each division would be responsible for manning its proportion of the seagoing fleet, Home and Foreign. He worked out in detail how this drastic change could be effected. He believed it would result in improved discipline through officers and men being together much more frequently, in a better standard of recommendations for advancement and assessments of ability, due to more intimate knowledge of and interest in the men.

He anticipated that each division would have an *esprit de corps*, which could last as long as itself and could be manifested in a multitude of ways beneficial to the general service, but that no larger loyalties would be disturbed as there would not be two ships in the same squadron manned by the same division. Divisional loyalty would not compete with squadron or fleet loyalty.

From his detailed examination he concluded that the scheme would necessitate a slight reduction in complements of ships and of ships in commission, but was prepared to accept this.

> In peace-time [he wrote] these affairs should be deliberate, scraping together a crew for such-and-such a ship is not a good augury for a commission. Hitherto the tendency has been to subordinate the good of the service to the requirements of the administrative machine. Rather should the machine adapt itself to the needs of the Fleet.

In conclusion he wrote :

> Our best and indeed our only bulwark against any of the tendencies of today that go to undermine law and order is the fuller recognition by the Officers of " Noblesse Oblige ", and that, when a condition of mutual trust and respect between officers and men has been attained in a ship, administration shall make it possible for it to be carried on as far as humanly is possible.

His proposals were not adopted and, if they ever were examined by the Admiralty Departments, it is probable that either it was not considered that there was a sufficiently strong case for such an upheaval, or that the scheme was not workable for reasons that had escaped Fisher's notice. But interest attaches to them, as they show that, though Fisher was steeped in tradition, he was prepared to jettison any process, however sanctified by long usage, if it was not attuned to modern conditions.

As to (*c*) he wanted to see a higher conception of duty permeating all ranks. He thought it a mistake to assume that the regulations governing service, training, advancement, conditions of life, pay, punishment, were at fault. " I think it is we who have been at fault, not the regulations, and tinkering with print will not remedy matters."

He believed that, if a captain made his officers do their duty, a higher state of morale or discipline could be inculcated in a man-of-war than would be found anywhere else. He came to the conclusion that, in order to make the "private-life" of each ship the "best possible", occasional periods of isolation were necessary, and that when the Fleet collected this "private-life" should be intruded on as little as possible. He stressed the value of independent cruises for ships of the Fleet.

Whilst emphasising the importance of maintaining the efficiency of the Fleet for battle, he, nevertheless, gave equal emphasis to the importance of leaving sufficient time for captains and officers to examine quietly and systematically the structure of discipline and morale on which technical proficiency rests.

In a large Fleet maintained on a basis of instant readiness for a war with a first-class naval power, such time may not be available, but unless that is the condition a period of "going rather slower" would be beneficial.

He recommended more attention being paid to ceremonials ; the teaching of and provision of opportunities for the art of command by petty and subordinate officers ; occasional informal lectures by officers on the traditions of the service and exploits of great seamen, in olden and recent times ; as much as possible of the technical instruction to be done by officers ; very careful supervision of gunnery and general drills.

> In general [he wrote] I feel that officers today carry their Anglo-Saxon reticence too far. It would be worse if they were too garrulous and always "improving the occasion", but unless they come out of their shells a bit more, they are not doing all they might. They are too modest and diffident. The sailor is very easily swayed even by men whom he instinctively distrusts. If no one ever talks to him except "on service" he turns the more readily to other counsellors, as we have seen. With such obviously impressionable material, it is a reflection on us that the hold on our men was not everywhere such as to meet the test it was put to recently. In the training establishments, young ratings are made very conscious

of the dignity and traditions of the service. On coming to sea these appear somewhat dim and only the remarkable boy can retain his first impressions in the hustle of life on the lower deck. Once such psychological values are lost, they are difficult to regain, and my main contention is that we must keep these things more in sight, preventing them from being submerged in the press of an exacting routine.

. . . . . .

We must hold together, I think, not on a new policy, but on a clearly restated old one, " the good of the service ". With right leadership we can not only regain our lost position — we can do much more than that — we can make the service an example of steadiness and loyalty the value of which in the days ahead may well be felt outside the boundaries of the Navy.

His somewhat revolutionary scheme for instituting Divisions could not have been received with approbation by all the officers of the Fleet, but in these remarks on raising the tone of the personnel he enunciated enduring principles which cannot be repeated too often.

During 1931, Chatfield, who was the First Sea Lord Designate, and the First Sea Lord had agreed that Fisher should succeed to the command when Chatfield hauled down his flag. In order that he should have six months' respite from the Mediterranean climate before a further three years on the station, Fisher handed over his duties as Second in Command to Sir Roger Backhouse in April 1932, and returned to England.

So ended a period of his career which was distinguished by his beneficial influence on the training of the Fleet for war and by his example of wise and vigorous leadership which set a new standard for many of the leaders of the future.

COMMANDER-IN-CHIEF, MEDITERRANEAN

WATCHING SHIPS ENTERING VALETTA HARBOUR

CHAPTER X

1932-1937

Commander-in-Chief, Mediterranean Fleet — Interest in the Maltese — Cruise in the Levant — Combined Fleet Manœuvres, 1934 — The Night Attack — Cruises in Adriatic — A great Ambassador — Royal Review at Spithead — Italian Crisis — Concentration of British Fleet at Alexandria — Commander-in-Chief, Portsmouth

FISHER hoisted his flag as Commander-in-Chief in the *Resolution* on 31st October, as the flagship *Queen Elizabeth* was due for refit, and Chatfield returned in her to England. He was at once in a whirl of work and calls, but a day seldom passed without a game of tennis or racquets. Three weeks later he was able to say that he had seen nearly every officer and man in the Fleet somehow or somewhere, either at parades, on shore, or in their ships. His energy was immense, and, though he had only just assumed command, he was looking forward to the visit of a French squadron early in December, which meant large dinner parties and a dance of 300. He was very pleased that the French suggested they should visit him first, as he thought it wrong for the British Commander-in-Chief always to call first on the French and Italian Commanders-in-Chief.

An early engagement was a dinner given him by the Maltese community. He had a great affection for the Maltese and, when Second in Command, had strongly supported the Commander-in-Chief when the latter, undeterred by the failure of several ex-Governors and Commanders-in-Chief, made a fresh attempt to induce the Union Club to admit Maltese to membership, and succeeded. The sturdy and isolated inhabitants of the village of Mgarr attracted his attention one day and he frequently visited them and became a fairy godfather to the village children.

Despite his many preoccupations when handing over the command three and a half years later to his successor, he did not forget his child friends in the secluded village :

DEAR FATHER SALOMONE,

Will you bring my child friends from Mgarr to tea (with hundreds of them possibly) on board *Queen Elizabeth* at about 4.50 P.M. on Monday 23rd March ? We shall sail at 7 P.M. for England. I shall count to see you and Maria and Giuseppe, Teresa etc. Bring a bus full for which a cheque enclosed.

Nor did he forget them when far away at Portsmouth :

DEAR FATHER SALOMONE,

This is our wedding day [December 21st]. Lady Fisher and I send a pound each for you to spend on our Little Friends at Mgarr — in any way that you choose.

News of Fisher's death threw all Mgarr into mourning. A street was renamed Fisher Street, and in June 1938 his successor, Admiral Sir Dudley Pound, unveiled a memorial tablet subscribed for by the villagers. In his address Father Salomone said :

It will be our happy privilege and duty to tell our visitors as we do today and to hand down to our future Mgarr — aye, to all who point interrogatively to this inscription — the ever fresh and gladdening story of how Sir William Fisher truly loved the lowly farmers of this secluded and far-flung parish. How he encouraged, petted, entertained and specially wanted near him in his big ship their poor little ones, the Giuseppes, the Teresas, and Carmelas.

But, though Mgarr occupied a special place in his affections, he was known and deeply respected the whole length or breadth of Malta. Every shopkeeper in Valetta looked forward to his cheery greeting as he strode through the streets, never forgetting a face. His unobtrusive kindnesses were many. One of the best known of the Malta lace-makers was Carmela Cassar. Her husband died and she fell dangerously ill. When she was on the road to recovery, Fisher with his two sons went to see her and begged her to come to Admiralty House next day, which was Christmas Day, and hear the King's Speech on the wireless, and told her not to be shy as there would be no one but the family and twelve senior officers, who all knew her well. How proud and pleased he would have been when the world was deeply stirred by the courage and endurance of the Maltese under continual heavy air attack! He had been an inspiration to both old and young and, in the words of his friend, the parish priest, had " knit the big hearts of a small people to Britannia, the pride of the ocean ".

In the spring of 1933 he went to Toulon to return the French Commander-in-Chief's visit and had what he called a " terrific visit with lunches, Thés Dansants, Soirées de Gala, Grand Bals in rapid succession ", which he enjoyed all the more as Lady Fisher and his daughter, Ros, were able to join in the festivities. From Toulon he went to Gibraltar to meet the *Queen Elizabeth*, now refitted, and there shifted his flag. There followed a stay at Golfe Juan, where the family were reunited, as his sons, Nevil and Charles, joined him.

In June he took the whole Fleet to the Eastern part of his command and much enjoyed visits to Egypt, Syria, and Greece, after a period of strenuous Fleet exercises and firings. His family were able to join him for these visits in the yacht *Bryony*. They never lost an opportunity of seeing interesting places or people. He wrote from Beyrout :

We are just finishing a pretty arduous visit here. Dinner parties and dances in considerable heat, but some have taken place in the mountains nearby which give quite a different climate, 4000-6000 feet up. Cecile, Ros, and I did a two days' tour *en route* to Baalbeck and Damascus, the former splendid. Temples that beat the Acropolis. The latter disappointing, though we saw the Tomb of John the Baptist, the street that is called Straight, St. Paul's house and Saladin's tomb, etc. But the drive to those places is what one remembers. The Lebanon Mountain ; the great fertile plains, the vivid colours, stretches of barrenness and then a wonderful oasis with ice-cold water and high shady trees, winding passes and gorges — a long string of Bedouin Arabs on 40 or 50 camels. We stop and they all gather round the car. The children slither down from their camels and kiss our hands, showers of piastres in return. A sensation of warm lips, cheeks and flashing eyes and we go on. This afternoon we are being taken for a final great expedition — one thinks nothing of motoring to a place 150 miles away.

A letter written from Navarin, where the *Queen Elizabeth* anchored in October, also gives an interesting picture of Fisher's life during the periods between the more serious work of training the Fleet :

Am in this historic harbour with my whole Fleet, proud and cosy. Cecilia and Ros cruising in the Gulf of Corinth, visiting Delphi, Mycenae, Missolonghi, etc. Nevil went off from Athens. Nevil and I had a very memorable early morning partridge shoot in Cyprus — starting at dark and watching the dawn — chill — and then hot sun. We had two days on a mountain in a sort of wooden Chalet Hotel 600 ft. high at Mt. Olympus. Athens was a scream. Ciss. and Ros going great guns and having arrived in *Bryony* three days before I got there in *Queen Elizabeth*, they were in the big Athens society whirl when we met. Dinners, dances, night clubs, etc. Athens is thoroughly demoralised anyhow when the Fleet is there. They dine at 10 P.M., that is if they do dine — but often it is a cocktail party which, starting about 8 P.M., lasts till 1 A.M. and then all go to a Cabaret. I didn't compete with that sort of thing. . . .

The annual programme of the Mediterranean Fleet

had been for many years governed by certain recurring commitments. In the spring the Home Fleet and Mediterranean met for manœuvres and, afterwards, proceeded to Gibraltar, where meetings were held to discuss the lessons learnt and the opportunity was taken for the staffs to discuss the many problems that had emerged during the previous year. Then there were periodical diplomatic visits to foreign countries, an annual visit to Egypt, and, in the interests of efficiency, every ship had to spend a part of the year away from Malta, and the gay life of cities, in the more isolated anchorages in Greek waters. Periods at Malta between cruises were necessary for refitting and restoring the ships, carrying out some of the gunnery practices, completing the Annual Musketry Course for the ships' companies, and so as to collect the whole Fleet for drills, inspections, the annual sports, and also give the personnel the opportunity of seeing their families.

With Fisher in command, life at Malta was never dull. In matters of custom and tradition he was strictly orthodox, but he liked to spring an unorthodox exercise on his officers and men and, now that he was Commander-in-Chief, he was able to exercise his fancy to the full. On one occasion when the Fleet was entering Malta after a long cruise, he made a signal ordering certain ships to complete forthwith with fuel, stores, provisions, water, and ammunition, and to signal when complete. The officers and men, whose thoughts had been centred on the prospects of seeing their families and once again enjoying the comparative delights of Malta, were at once agog to know where trouble had arisen, and all hands worked like niggers and finished the job by midnight, to find that they were not leaving Malta after all, and that it was their imaginative Commander-in-Chief satisfying himself that, if an emergency arose, his ships could be prepared in a certain time. On another occasion he took two officers into his confidence and told them to simulate foreign agents and board a ship just before midnight, and go through the " motions " of wrecking her. There were always plenty of surprises and plenty of fun wherever he was, but a serious purpose usually lay behind the unexpected orders.

The annual manœuvres did not as a rule attract public attention, but those of 1934 will never be forgotten by anyone who was present and the press correspondents' accounts appeared in the daily papers under banner headlines. They set the seal on Fisher's reputation as a brilliant and fearless tactician. In earlier chapters his habit of exercising his ships at high speed in very close order has been noted and also his work with Lord Chatfield in the development of night fighting. Now he was to have a chance of putting his training to a practical test. The object of the Home Fleet was to escort transports to a landing-place, somewhere on a 400-mile coastline represented by the Spanish-Portuguese coast; Fisher's object was to frustrate the landing. The Commander-in-Chief, Home Fleet, faced with a difficult situation, tried to draw his opponent away from the convoy by sending his battle cruisers on a southern route, whilst he took a northern route. In the early stages a gale blew up and aircraft, of which Fisher had a superiority, could not fly, and the Home Fleet destroyers, who were caught in a violent secondary disturbance, had to leave the battle area for shelter in Lagos. The battle cruisers were the first " enemy " ships sighted by one of Fisher's far-flung patrol line of cruisers, destroyers, and submarines, but almost immediately a cruiser sighted and reported the enemy battle fleet and transports. Fisher decided at once to proceed at highest speed and bring the enemy battle fleet to action during the night, and before the battle cruisers could reinforce. High seas were running but Fisher pressed on with no lights showing and about midnight sighted his quarry and swung his ships into battle line at a range of 6000 yards, switching on searchlights and filling the sky with star-shell. "The moment was spectacular beyond even the dreams of the most ambitious Hollywood producer", wrote a correspondent. This extract from a letter written by H. A. L. Fisher, who joined his brother after the manœuvres, is of interest:

William was looking splendidly well and fit and much satisfied with his brilliant victory in the manœuvres when he smashed his enemy in a midnight battle in a terrific gale which lasted six days, during which William never went to bed. It is regarded by all the experts as an epoch-making achievement and very daring, for William was steaming at 16 knots against the enemy in the darkest of nights, every ship with its lights concealed, until the moment came to light up and show the Home Fleet that they were surrounded.

Fisher was hailed by the press as the greatest naval genius of modern times. The First Sea Lord, Sir Ernle Chatfield, wrote:

It must have given you the greatest satisfaction after all your hard work and original thought about night actions, to have had such a wonderful opportunity and the courage and skill to carry it out under the weather conditions. I am sure it has greatly increased the prestige of the Fleet in the eyes of the public, who will now realise that there are some places other than the English Channel and North Sea where our Fleets may have to fight.

The Fleets returned to Gibraltar. For several years past it had been the custom to assemble all the officers of the two Fleets in the great shed on the Mole for the purpose of describing and discussing the manœuvres. One of the Chiefs of Staff read the narrative; the junior flag officers, senior officers of destroyers, and captains of ships that had been detailed then corrected any mistakes in the narrative, submitted their views on the events, and gave their reasons for the course of action they had adopted; and finally the two Commanders-in-Chief summed up and extracted the lessons that had been learnt. In past years a summing-up by a Commander-in-Chief had often left a profound effect on his listeners and had exercised a permanent influence on tactical and strategical thought.

So the officers were looking forward eagerly to Fisher's final speech. They were to be disappointed, as the Commanders-in-Chief opened the proceedings themselves and each gave a narrative of events from his point of view. The reason given for departure from the usual programme was that some of the Board of Admiralty were present and, as they had much to see, time could not be spared for a discussion. This was not very convincing, as all knew that if Fisher had wished for a discussion there would have been one. They also knew well the importance Fisher attached to full discussion and giving the junior officers a chance of expressing their views. Then the truth dawned on them. There could be no criticism of Fisher's strategy and tactics ; they had been perfect. So any discussion or criticism would revolve round his opponent's strategy. In the hour of a great triumph Fisher revealed the full measure of his generous nature. It is interesting to note that Admiral Sir Andrew Cunningham was present, being then Rear-Admiral commanding the destroyer flotillas, and the ships of his command had no small part in bringing about with precision the situation designed by his Commander-in-Chief.

In July, Fisher, when staying at the hotel on Mt. Troodos in Cyprus, received news that British officers had been fired on by the Turks at Samos and one had been killed :

> I collected every ship I could lay my hands on, 2 Battleships, 3 Cruisers, 7 Destroyers, and went full speed for Samos. It was the sight of all those ships within 36 hours at the very spot that brought the Turks to reason. For they were very

haughty and uppish till we appeared and refused to allow British boats to search for the body of the shot officer. That was altered after I got there. The Memorial Service close in to the Turkish coast, was impressive, and I made the Turkish Destroyer anchor close to the Q.E., and they dropped a beautiful big wreath as we fired our volleys over the spot.

Fisher liked the Turks, but would allow no one to flout the British flag.

In October he was at Split taking part in the first funeral ceremonies of the King of Yugoslavia, who had been assassinated. He was much impressed by the singing of the Slav choirs and the obvious grief of the 50,000 people who came in from the countryside and were most of them in tears. He said to the Ban of Split, "You can organise almost anything, but you cannot organise grief like this." The Ban repeated the words to the peasants who were passing at the moment and they were passed from mouth to mouth through the country and reached the ears of our Minister at Belgrade. "When the train left," he wrote, "a paroxysm of grief and parting cries as for a friend who had gone. It occurred to me that one could die for a boy King but not a Dictator." He went to Belgrade for the funeral and there found Marshal Pétain and General Goering amongst the foreign representatives. The Duke of Kent, General Braithwaite, and Fisher went at 9 A.M. to the Villa where the King's body was lying in state, to lay our King's wreath, but as they arrived there was a stampede and Pétain and his officers rushed in so as to be first. The British Navy was given the most prominent place and 100 sailors marched in the procession.

He was particularly fond of visiting the Adriatic Eastern seaboard and made many friends there. In Bruce Lockhart's *Guns or Butter* there is an interesting reference to one of these visits and the impression Fisher left on the people :

Orebic was the favourite resort of the late Admiral Sir William Fisher, when he was Commander-in-Chief of the Mediterranean Fleet. He did not come there to hunt jackals but to take exercise. Every day he landed and walked along the coast for two or three hours. He had, as companions, the Mayor of Orebic, and an ex-captain who had sailed the Seven Seas and who spoke English. The Admiral not only took his exercise. He discussed with rare desire for information every aspect of local politics and every problem of the Adriatic. The Mayor, who had never walked so far in his life, was immensely impressed, and now Sir William Fisher's name is more respected than any other in Orebic. Because of the world reputation which the British Navy enjoys, British Admirals, who take an intelligent interest in human affairs, can do more for Britain than a whole train-load of peripatetic ministers.

The same could have been written of every place that he visited. He always made friends with the inhabitants, was always interested in their lives, and they treasured the memory of the tall, distinguished Admiral with the gracious manner, who walked through the streets exchanging greetings with all and sundry. He was a very welcome visitor to Corfu, and the Corfiots always rushed to the landing-place to greet him when they saw the familiar green barge approaching the shore.

The arrival of the British Fleet at Corfu is always received with warm enthusiasm. Particularly, though, the Commander-in-Chief, Sir W. Fisher, who is a recognised Philhellene and friend of the island, constitutes for the Corfiots a wholly exceptional personality and is surrounded by the unanimous and sincere affection of the Corfu people. The Fleet of no other nation enjoys the love of Corfu as much as the British, as the British remind us of the imposing strength which saved us from a peril the consequence of which still remains profoundly engraved on our hearts. These few lines represent the sincere sentiment of every Corfiot, and are addressed to the British sailors and especially to their distinguished leader, the Commander-in-Chief of the British Power in the Mediterranean.

Thus wrote the editor of a Corfu paper.

It was always the same wherever Fisher went. He was a great Ambassador.

The year 1935 was Jubilee Year and Fisher was delighted when he was told that the Mediterranean Fleet was to take part in a great Naval Review at Spithead. " The King reviews the Navy at Spithead on July 16th, and I shall be there. It will be a corking affair and one of the supreme ambitions of my life will be satisfied for I shall be head cook."

He was apprehensive that trouble was brewing in the Mediterranean but he had prepared for all eventualities, and he was satisfied that the absence of the Fleet for the short period of the Review would not influence the course of events.

After the Fleet had anchored, the Royal yacht anchored at the head of the line and the flag officers went on board for audience of the King. A naval contemporary of Fisher's, who was a guest in the *Queen Elizabeth*, was, like everyone else on board, struck by Fisher's appearance when he came on deck :

> Fisher presented a noble and, to many, a moving sight as he, in his full dress with the red riband of the Grand Cross of the Bath, went over the side and down into his barge to the salute of his officers and the playing of " Rule, Britannia ", which is the salute to a naval Commander-in-Chief.

He had received the G.C.B. in the Birthday Honours, and, during the Review, the King conferred on him the G.C.V.O.

After the Review, Fisher led the Fleet to sea to carry out a programme of gunnery exercises, which were watched by the King from the Royal yacht. Lord Jellicoe wrote :

> I am just back in London from the Review and Exercises, and feel that I must write to congratulate you most heartily on

(1) The very fine organisation of everything connected with the two days.
(2) The handling of the Fleet.
(3) The fine target practice.

It must be a matter of great satisfaction to you to know that everything went so well and that the approaching termination of your command afloat was marked by so great an event.

But the thoughts of many of those who witnessed that impressive Review and took part in the Jubilee celebrations were often wandering from the peaceful gay scenes to the Mediterranean, where Mussolini and his confederates had driven and cajoled the peace-loving Italian people to believe that it was their destiny to re-found a Roman Empire. Soon after Fisher's return to the Mediterranean, the tension over Italy's attack on Abyssinia called for naval preparations of a comprehensive kind. It was fortunate for the country that a man of Fisher's powers was in command. The grievous shortage in equipment and reserves, resulting from years of economy, had to be made good in haste.

For strategical reasons Fisher concentrated his Fleet at Alexandria, where there were few facilities for recreation for officers and men kept month after month under the strain of quasi-war conditions, and so a heavy burden of organisation and improvisation fell upon the Commander-in-Chief. His undefeated spirit communicated itself to all under his command. Every officer and man had complete confidence in him. The discipline of all ratings remained throughout those wearing months at the highest level.

In September he wrote that he had masses of telegrams and reports and the most difficult arrangements to make and that elaborating the machinery for war was so much more trying than the use of it. But he did not believe that it would be used.

He was very impressed with Sir Samuel Hoare's speech

and his Geneva broadcast, which he considered " first rate and takes the big British attitude of dignity and courage ".

He anticipated that, after Italy had commenced her march into Abyssinia, there would be talks of the type of export that would be stopped to her and that events would move slowly. He had to endure, day after day, the sight of the Italian transports passing his Fleet :

Egyptians friendly, and all quiet on shore. When an Italian transport passes through, all the soldiers are drilled to shout " Duce, Duce, Duce " and occasionally a party of the local Italians are organised to shout back, adding " Abyssinia a noi ", etc. I see a lot of RA(D) [1] who lies close to us, and he is a great trump.

A few days later he wrote :

Watched a large Italian transport bound for Abyssinia (two or three every day). The men were massed on deck and singing and cheering whilst motor cars followed abreast of them on the road waving flags and cheering. We felt rather out of it ! They saw my green barge with white ensign alongside a landing stage. Were silent for a moment and then went on cheering the procession ashore. These poor Italian soldiers (for they are being driven by Mussolini) seem so anxious for English sympathy ! As an instance, we had all the boys on a picnic up the Canal. A big trooper passed very close and the Petty Officer told all the boys to keep quite still. One however waved his hand gaily. Immediately there was a storm of cheers from the Italians ! What a funny business it all is.

Despite the press of work he seldom missed his daily game of tennis. The Vice-Admiral, Charles Forbes, and the Captain of the Fleet, Captain Whitworth, and Richard Coleridge, a lieutenant who was engaged to his daughter Ros, often made up the four :

Tennis with dear old Charles Forbes (who is *golden* and such a cheerful help) against Whitworth and Richard 2 sets

[1] Rear-Admiral A. B. Cunningham.

all. *Great* fun. I asked Richard whether he had any news from Malta, especially by that clever flying boat. He said yes and that Ros had a temperature and was in bed. So he had wired and now knew that temperature was normal, and R back to duty. I could have hugged the dear fellow.

Lady Fisher and her daughter were working hard at Malta in anticipation of war with Italy. There were many sailors' wives there and much to be organised that came in their province. Fisher was anxious for the wives with children to leave the island at once and wished a scheme prepared to evacuate the remainder from the harbour area into the country if war appeared imminent:

It's no good having a false bravery [he wrote] and sticking it out at this most dangerous spot, when you can avoid it and make reasonably certain that you will be alive and well to work and care for others the next day.

By October he had come to the conclusion that France would not support " anything worth calling a sanction ", and that though both Italy and ourselves were preparing at full speed, we would not make war and it was hardly conceivable that Italy would declare war on us.

Alexandria was proving a poor place as a large fleet base:

The sporting club is bright and gay and the teas are good. Grass lawn — large umbrellas — but the females — my hat! If ever there was a place more devoid of soul than Alexandria I should like to see it — or rather not to see it.

You never see a nice face — man or woman. Whilst we were at dinner this evening on the Quarter Deck the *Bulldog*'s boat's crew were towed past. *Bulldog* had just won the 4th Flotilla Regatta. They cheered like mad and sang " He's a jolly good fellow " and " Boys of the Bulldog breed " — gave a comfy feeling in the pit of the tummy. Dear fellows. They are having a dull time, no night leave and no grouses and a lot of hard work.

At the end of October he wrote to the First Sea Lord :

All is well. Very well I think in spite of restricted leave, and a great deal of hard work, poor recreational facilities and fabulous price of beer. There has been no grumbling, on the contrary great keenness. We keep up our programmes of exercises and firings just as if we were at Malta. Every day and most nights squadrons and flotillas are at sea and so far we have managed to get in and out of this congested harbour without incident. Yesterday I counted 84 ships and vessels under my orders in Alexandria alone. Air attacks on the fleet in harbour and at sea, day and night, all days except Saturday and Sunday. I get more glad every day that Dudley Pound came out — we can discuss things so openly together and never disagree, and his orderly and logical mind is a great example to the Staff.

Admiral Sir Dudley Pound was to have relieved Fisher in October but when the crisis came the Admiralty decided to leave Fisher in command. Pound then obtained the First Sea Lord's permission to offer his services as Chief of Staff, which was gladly accepted.

No one could be a better showman than Fisher when it was in the interests of the country to stage a dramatic display. It was, in his view, important that the world and the Egyptians should have no doubts about the strength of the British Fleet at Alexandria and its immediate readiness for war. One of these demonstrations was witnessed by an American reporter whose telegram caused him much amusement :

Biggest guns in British Navy fifteen inches hurling thousands of tons hot metal ten miles and more through air went to work this afternoon in Eastern Mediterranean in the greatest naval show ever staged off this port since the British blew the stink off its back in eighteen hundred and four.

English High Commissioner for Egypt Sir Miles Lampson and Admiral Sir W. W. Fisher commanding British Naval Forces, Mediterranean, presented this impressive, ear-shattering exhibition of John Bull's might for carefully selected audience composed representatives Egyptian Royal Family Prime Minister's Cabinet Ministers ex-Ministers and Egyptian notables former officials and the only American newspaper correspondent who has been permitted to observe British Navy actually firing long-range projectiles at targets. British Admiralty London sidestepped my cable request for visitation and Lampson said he couldn't think of such a thing and Admiral Fisher turned me down so flat I bounced but I managed crash party by mistake because happened be wearing English hat replacing yank lost with Italian Army in Ethiopia.

Show started shortly before noon some fifteen twenty miles outside Alexandria Sun bright brisk breeze choppy sea running over blue Mediterranean causing destroyers roll pitch decks awash but British gunners rubber boots to knees and bare from waist up exposing flamboyant tattooing manned guns and slammed out shells bracketing target-sending jets white water high air all round target which towed with five hundred foot line by auxiliary steamer in which I would not liked to have been.

Our glasses then picked up new arrivals steaming up over horizon out of grey-blue mists. First they appeared vague indistinct in distance their blue grey and darker slate grey colouring merging them both with sky and sea.

Finally they materialised as five of Britain's mightiest men-of-war five large battleships in line ahead led by flagship *Queen Elizabeth* flying flag Admiral Fisher. Following came *Barham Valiant* and *Ramillies* all England heaviest and toughest-looking bulldogs of the sea.

Salvo after salvo of shells one ton each and landing in groups of twenty at a time four guns from each of the five battleships firing at a time salvo after salvo continued to keep sea in constant tormented upheaval.

Silence that followed five minutes this continuous rapid firing so thick you could cut it with knife but it was gradually disturbed by distant indistinct droning from overhead high above in apparently empty sky of fleecy white clouds against blue ceiling of Mediterranean. The drone increased to buzz and suddenly changed to roar as squadron after squadron of speedy fighter planes and bombers were diving with motors full and broke through screen of white cloud and descended like swarm of bees not only on line British Battleships but also on two cruisers carrying distinguished Egyptian guests whose red Tarboosh capped heads soon bobbing about all neck twisting directions black silken fez tassels swinging all ways as owners ducked and finally shook heads in bewilderment surrender this unexpected demonstration potential destruction.

It was fitting nerve tinglish conclusion to this dramatic rehearsal of what Britain holds in store here in Alexandria harbour for whatever power that threatens the Suez Canal jugular vein and roadway Empire East and West. There's fifty thousand men and four hundred thousand tons of steelclad dynamite waiting here with guns loaded and steam up and decks cleared for action. It's certainly going to be hell if it's ever turned loose.

On another day he organised a great parade of seamen on shore, followed by a march through the city, which left a deep impression on the onlookers. Some years before, he had urged the Governor of Cyprus to allow a similar march of armed men through Nicosia, when the situation looked ugly, but unfortunately the Governor did not appreciate the value of such a demonstration, which might well have prevented the subsequent rioting and burning of Government House.

In the midst of this press of work and responsibility, he received news of his son Nevil's death in a flying accident. He summoned up all his reserve of courage and faith and met the grievous blow by throwing himself with still greater energy into his work. A month earlier he had written:

It's great news about Nevil. I sent him a cable to say how delighted I was at his *right decision* to join such a glorious service. I'm sure he will be terribly happy and a great man in it.

His friend, Maurice Baring, wrote these lines about Nevil, which appeared in the *Sunday Times*:

Upon life's threshold ; gallant, gay and shy
He flew into his heritage, the sky.
To those who here must mourn him for a while
He left behind him an undying smile.

The day after he received news of Nevil's death his judgment in an emergency and power of making rapid decisions were put to high test. Shortly after Colours were hoisted, the *Ausonia*, a large Italian liner, entered the harbour, and when almost abreast the flagship burst into flames. It was a tense moment. To every one of the thousands who were watching her the same thought occurred. Was she carrying a cargo of explosives? Fisher's mind was made up the moment he saw the flames. In a few minutes boats of his flagship were racing to the doomed liner to rescue the passengers and crew.

"Tubby" Clayton, founder padre of Toc H, came to Alexandria to reinforce the naval chaplains, and it was not long before he and the chaplains were busy planning to meet the urgent need for a sailors' club in Alexandria, which was entirely lacking in properly-run hotels where the sailors could get good beer and a good meal at a reasonable price and meet their friends. Fisher was at once whole-heartedly in favour of Clayton's project, and backed it with all his authority. "Claridge's Fleet Club", wrote Clayton, "could never have begun if the C in C had not with instant vision flung his whole might into it. It took a great original Commander to implement with every emphasis a step for which there was no precedent at all, except in Talbot House in Flanders Days."

With Fisher and Clayton behind the project the dream was soon a reality and as many as 4000 men could be seen there in an evening, dancing, playing games, listening to concerts, writing their letters home, and drinking good beer.

Another tribute to Fisher's character written by Clayton at this time may be quoted. After describing how the City of Silver Grey, as he called the Fleet, assembled, he went on :

The City of Silver Grey has good-humoured citizens. In this, as in all else their C-in-C never denied his men the magic of his understanding. His was a human touch which spurned any awkwardness. Deeper than that, he had what Paul calls charity, and tales against himself formed part of it. One night the masters and chiefs of oilers, store ships, and other ships not to be specified were bidden to the table of " tall Agrippa ". Later, their host arose and told his guests that on that very morning he had been to a hospital ship, and therein found a most diminutive patient, aged 14. The boy, small for his years, was from a tanker, where he was steward's boy. Questioned by Agrippa, he was compelled to admit that he had not tempted Neptune hitherto. " But what," said tall Agrippa with assumed solemnity, " what do you suppose that your ship is doing without you ? " " God knows, Sir," said the boy with unexpected piety.

The crisis past, neither our Government nor the people were prepared to go to war single-handed on an issue that concerned all the signatories of the League Covenant, so Mussolini proceeded unhindered with the conquest of the weakly-armed Abyssinians, and started the series of aggressive attacks on peaceful peoples that culminated in the outbreak of the Second World War.

But not an officer or man in the Mediterranean Fleet doubted that if Great Britain had declared war they would find themselves in the right place at the right time to inflict the maximum destruction on the Italian Fleet.

Whilst at Alexandria, Fisher kept in the closest touch with the situation in Egypt and won the sincere friendship of the Egyptian leaders. He liked the Egyptians and they liked him and would take from him frank opinions on Egypt's strategical dependence on the British Navy which they might have resented from others.

His personal influence undoubtedly played a large part in the negotiations which eventually resulted in the

Anglo-Egyptian Treaty and in greatly improved relations between Egypt and ourselves. " Latterly there have been the Treaty discussions," wrote Sir Miles Lampson, " and I and all members of our Delegation most deeply regret your departure. It will be a great loss to all of us, both official and personal."

By the end of March 1936 the tension had relaxed and Fisher handed over the command to Sir Dudley Pound. Some weeks before the First Lord had offered him the Portsmouth Command, which he had some hesitation in accepting :

> I do so highly appreciate the compliment [he wrote], but I had genuine hesitation because there are so few places to go round and I feel I have had a great deal more than my share. This last command of mine satisfies me *to the brim* — I should jolly well think so ! — and before my Foreign Service leave is expired almost, I drop straight into another job. I hope the Service will forgive me — it looks so grasping but I couldn't find a way of saying No without making everyone uncomfortable and being thought a humbug.

He had a magnificent send-off. " It was touching the way in which they all clamoured to shake his hand for the last time ", wrote one of the officers.

After a farewell dinner in the *Renown*, the Admirals rowed him back to the *Queen Elizabeth* in the galley, escorted by a double-banked cutter, manned by the captains. As the *Queen Elizabeth*, with the Admiral's silk flag at the main, steamed slowly out of harbour next morning, each ship in turn saluted and cheered, as never before, the tall figure of their great leader standing on top of the forward turret.

He called at Malta on passage home :

> We had (he wrote) a terrific six hours at Malta in cold, rather blowy weather. First of all I had to do two big inspections at Manoel Island, destroyers, submarines, and mine-sweeper crews. Speeches ! My hat ! Then to old Mrs. Price

— who was in bed but jolly buckish. Then to Casino Maltese for a Vin d'honneur at noon. About 500 people there. Another speech. Three cheers, etc., — then to Luke for lunch. Then, to save my life, 40 minutes squash with Basil Hood at J.O.C., then a tea party at home on Quarter Deck to *all* Malta — ranging from Lord Strickland to Maltese children without boots — I roped in everyone I could think of. You couldn't get about it was so crowded ; six to seven hundred I should say.

At 6.30 we pushed them all off and sailed at 7. St. Angelo floodlit. Destroyers anchored inside and just clear of the fair-way unknown to us, and as we passed they suddenly switched on illuminations and were found to be crammed with matelots — more cheering, and frightfully effective and neatly done. Breakwaters and Barraccas joined in and the " Q.E.'s " felt that they had had a royal send-off.

He hoisted his flag in the *Victory* at Portsmouth on 7th July 1936, and looked forward to a happy three years with his family round him but, though he was just as eager as ever for a daily game of tennis and seemed to have lost none of his vigour and enthusiasms, his immense output of energy at both work and play had left their mark on his constitution.

The preparations for the Coronation Naval Review fell on him and this, with the reception and entertain-ment of the foreign naval officers, over-burdened him.

He attended a reception given by the Speaker of the House of Commons one evening shortly before Coronation Day, and returned home very tired, but his great spirit enabled him to stand the strain of the day, and few realised that his strength was ebbing.

Indeed one of his friends, who was staying with him for the Review, wrote a few days later : " How splendid he looked in his Madder sash of the Bath and with a beauty of face which owes nothing to honours but to honour and the air of heaven ".

After the long ceremonies were over he knew he must

have a rest and he went to stay at the house of a friend near Salisbury. Then came the King's Birthday Review on Southsea Common. Nothing would stop him from taking the salute and, summoning up all his will power, he did the sixty-mile drive and appeared at the saluting base. But standing there at the salute overtaxed his waning strength and he nearly fainted.

After the Review, he returned to the country, his last duty done.

He died on 24th June 1937, at the age of sixty-two. He was buried at sea near the Nab Tower.

ON THE BRIDGE OF A DESTROYER WITH THE KING OF SPAIN

H.M.S. *QUEEN ELIZABETH* LEAVING ALEXANDRIA, HOMEWARD BOUND

CHAPTER XI

"*W. W*"

Admiral Sir William Fisher, or "W. W" as he was always known in the Navy, spent nearly half a century of unsparing endeavour and hard work in the service of the nation. The preceding chapters, it is hoped, may have afforded some insight into what the country and the Royal Navy owe to his untiring efforts. For he never spared himself from the day in 1888 when as a delicate, sensitive, scholarly boy he joined the *Britannia* to that crowning moment forty-eight years later when he stood on the fore-turret of the flagship of the Mediterranean Fleet and received the salute of thousands of officers and men who would have followed him anywhere—officers and men who cheered as they had never cheered before in an endeavour to convey to him all that was in their hearts.

My own most abiding recollection of him was when he passed by every morning on his way to his barge, waiting to take him to the Vice-Admiral's flagship lying in Valetta harbour.

His noble figure, his face lit up with the sheer pleasure of being alive under the Mediterranean sun, his keen eye missing nothing — not a stone, not a flower — of his beloved Malta, and his joyous shout, "Can anything be better than this?"

That, too, is the picture engraved on the minds of thousands of Maltese children who will one day tell their children about the tall Admiral who divested himself of all pomp and ceremony to come amongst them and share their joys and sorrows. The people of the now famous George Cross Island will never forget him.

Nor will those other Mediterranean peoples on the

Adriatic seaboard and in the Greek Islands who called him friend and eagerly awaited his coming.

From one aspect, what I have written in the earlier chapters is out of tune with the times. There is an old saying that critics are men who brush the coats of noblemen; it is the fashion today to wield the brush very vigorously. The eminent Victorians are removed from their eminence and we learn that, though they had some virtues, their vices were many.

Biographies containing some spice have a wider reading public than those portraying a man of unblemished life. But my diligent search through the material given me — his letters, private notes and memoranda — left me with nothing wherewith to fashion into clay some part of this man who was the idol of that great Fleet at Alexandria.

Let me explain. I have been privileged to read his private letters, in which there was no need for restraint, and I have found not one single note of disparagement of a brother officer. I thought perhaps that as a midshipman or sub-lieutenant — the age when we see so many imperfections in our seniors — he might have expressed his dislike or contempt for some of the officers. But no — he saw what was good in all of them.

So it was always, officers or men. In the *St. Vincent* he is leading "850 such gallant delightful souls" and there is "not one of the officers I would not trust to the bitter, bitter end". When a Rear-Admiral watching his men march past, he finds it the most moving thing he has ever seen, and the officers and men looking so magnificent that the lump will rise in his throat.

As I read letter after letter — all in his vivid, staccato style — I began to understand something that a friend of his had written shortly before he died and which I have already quoted: "How splendid he looked and with a beauty of face which owes nothing to honours but to honour and the air of heaven!"

Final understanding came to me before I had read them all. This was a man who had never borne malice, who, though conscious of his powers, had never let ambition become a demon to cloy the joy of being alive in a world that offered adventure and was full of lovely things — a man who had passed through life without once letting anger or excitement cause an injustice to an officer or sailor.

He was, I now knew, incapable of petty jealousies. More fortunate contemporaries might be distinguishing themselves in battle whilst he could see nothing ahead but a fruitless wait at Scapa — he would like to be with them, who wouldn't? — but he was always glad, truly glad, that they had had their chance.

So far, then, I had found no clay and I turned to the more intimate letters that were mainly about his family. They were, as I was expecting, characteristic and full of fun and amusing little drawings, full of eager inquiries when separated, bursting with happiness when reunited. The first letter I picked up was this:

" Divine. Walked to the sands. Not another soul there. All of us bathed. Ciss shouts " This is LIFE " — so it was. Nippy but the real thing. Ozone, sky, seagulls, and health. After tea we had a wonderful bike ride in hot sunshine. Saw Nelson's birth place. Such fields of corn and roots and partridges. Wet today but we are going out in macs on our bikes.

That was written when they were on holiday; all their days together were like that. In the last letter I found this:

I am going to Portsmouth on July 13th and we shall all then feel very close to one another. Somehow we must prevent Mungo choosing that moment to join the Mediterranean Fleet. Admiralty House would be unbearable without Racy and her children.

Looking back I find that I have not before mentioned

Racy's marriage to Mungo Buxton and how delighted her parents were and, more culpable, I find no mention of the arrival in the world of any of the children. Ros appears suddenly during those halcyon days at Plymouth but is already old enough to be a delight to her father when he returns from work ; Racy, Nevil, and Charles also appear out of the blue in some letter that I was not quoting for the purpose of introducing them. But I will let it be. I hesitated to quote more freely from these letters. They reveal all his glowing pride in his exceptionally good-looking children, his keen desire when away from home to know every little detail about them, the eagerness with which he looked forward to those joyful days together in the country for which he made such careful plans, his infinite trouble over the boys' education ; but they are written with that easy abandon of letters that are only meant for one person to read.

No clay so far, but there are other things than sterling character and a happy family life. That can be said of many men who lead irreproachable lives but miss most of the things that make life an epic adventure.

There is clay in a man who in unmoved by the beauties of nature, by music, by pictures, or by books because he is thereby a dull companion in any company and is lacking in the finer perceptions.

I think that one of the most remarkable things about Fisher was that, though he lived in a naval age when severe competition and the striving for ever-increasing efficiency conspired to narrow down the naval officer's interests to his ship and nothing beyond his ship, his interests widened with every year, and few men have extracted so much unalloyed pleasure from the beautiful things of this world.

For several decades before he joined the Navy, service on foreign stations was the common lot of officers and men ; the political horizon was usually clear of cloud, and, as we know from letters and autobiographies, life could be very pleasant. A ship's every movement was not reported by wireless, and if the captain thought he had found a good place for his officers and men he stayed there until its attractions began to wane, and then moved further up the coast. He would not think twice about leaving his ship for a week or more to visit a distant town or for a tour of the country, and would expect his officers to plan shooting trips and expeditions far afield.

But those pleasant days were brought to an end by the Kaiser and, by the time Fisher was a lieutenant, life in the Navy had become a stern business and, far from spending weeks up-country with rod and gun, officers thought themselves lucky if they snatched a few days' leave a year.

The ship might anchor off a town of great historic interest; the scrub-covered hillsides might be known to harbour red-legged partridges; near-by mountain-tops might be shouting a challenge to the adventurous; but in a few weeks' time there was the annual gunlayer's test on which the reputation of the ships hangs — there was no time to go ashore.

That was the way with many; an early love for the country and trees and birds and suchlike, which had blossomed in a home where these things counted for much, faded because the emotions were never stirred.

But Fisher's early love never faded; instead it grew stronger with time and with every fresh experience. Only a man whose senses were stabbed wide awake to nature's rich treasury could have written as he did about the Bosphorus and the Greek Islands, or discovered, as he always did, something arresting on a bleak northern waste-land.

It was tempting to quote more of those letters he wrote when in Mediterranean waters. Like a magic carpet they transport one for a moment to a world of hot blue skies, warm inviting sea, green valleys gay with blossom and friendly smiling peasants, and one can almost smell the fields and the flowers. Perhaps Wordsworth had something to do with that! Or perhaps the poet's sailor brother, John, who had the same gift of writing about nature and who bore a striking resemblance to him. When his travel days were over, he could truthfully say that he had never missed an opportunity of exploring a town or country that could be reached by hook or by crook.

If there was something that had been missed when he returned to his ship in the evening, he would be off again at first light of morning in the skiff. Not that he wished to enjoy it all alone. No man was ever more eager to share his pleasures with other men, and if duty kept him on board he would descend on the wardroom and gunroom and infect the officers with his enthusiasm and almost drive them ashore.

But how did he find the time for all this? He had to train his men for the forthcoming gunlayer's test, for the severe test of a Battle Practice, for the highly competitive evolutions; his ship had to be the cleanest ever and his men the smartest in the Fleet. Well, we know he did find time and that his ship was nearly always first in a very strong field. The answer is that there were no unforgiving minutes in his life. Look at that first letter from the *St. Vincent*, typical of so many. One moment he is diving into a turret to shake up a gun's crew, the next he is making out a programme for Team Marathon races; before the ink is dry, he is in a stokehold talking to the stokers about their work; during the next half hour he has what he calls "hand-on-arm" with the chief cook and the wireless petty officer, and we leave him organising a cricket match between officers and men.

A friend likened him to a whirlwind when he arrived at the Admiralty to deal with the submarine menace.

Tornado would be a better description of him when all his enthusiasm was roused : but it was sturdy young saplings, not wreckage, that he left in his track.

A successful career in a service in which there is keen competition for promotion depends, to some extent, on being the right man in the right place at the right time. For instance, a naval officer of the highest attainments may be serving on a station remote from a scene of hostilities, and when the periodic promotions come to be considered by the Selection Board, officers who have distinguished themselves in war inevitably, and with perfect justice, have the best chance of being selected. Again, an officer of great promise may find his chance of early promotion waning because there happen to be one or two officers, also of good reputation, in his ship who are senior to him and who will be recommended for promotion before him. There is thus a slight element of luck. But there are always a few officers in each generation who are universally recognised as being so outstanding that their rise in the service is assured. That Fisher was one of these was realised early in his career by his contemporaries in the Gunnery Lieutenant's Long Course. Though, as a young man, he was denied the opportunity given to more fortunate contemporaries of seeing active service in South Africa, China, and the Sudan, he was always " the right man in the right place at the right time " in the field of naval endeavour. He was selected to attend the " *Venerable* firings ", which established the principles of long-range naval gunnery ; he was first and gunnery lieutenant of the Atlantic Fleet flagship when he entered the promotion zone ; his first appointment as commander was to a ship that had fallen into slack ways, always a fine chance for a man of ability to make his name ; as flag commander to Sir William May, he played an important part in establishing tactical principles for the new high speed all-big-gun Fleet. But luck played no part in all this. It was his work as gunnery lieutenant of the *Canopus* that secured him the coveted appointment to the Senior Staff of the Gunnery School; his reputation stood so high that when Percy Scott impetuously dismissed him from the Senior Staff, the Commander-in-Chief of the Atlantic Fleet and his flag captain at once requested that he should be appointed first lieutenant of the new flagship — that dismissal would have wrecked the career of a lesser man; his work as first lieutenant led to his selection as commander of the *Albemarle* and subsequently to his selection for the important appointment of flag commander. Perhaps Lord Jellicoe's decision to retain him as captain of the *St. Vincent* when she ceased to be a flagship, whereby he became by far the youngest private battleship captain, was the most striking recognition of his outstanding ability.

He was an enthusiastic games player; cricket was his first love, and he never lost interest in the game. He took up rackets as a young lieutenant and, in later life, was a keen lawn tennis and squash player. When serving in the Mediterranean Fleet, hardly a day passed without a game of squash or tennis and, however busy he was, or however preoccupied with service matters, he somehow found time to relax and enjoy an hour's fresh air and exercise. With his physical fitness, long reach, and good eye, he could, I believe, have been in the first rank at some games if he had wished, but he was the last man to make a business of any form of recreation. It was all great fun to him. He played to win, but winning was not his exclusive object, and he was by temperament unsuited to devoting the time to practice that is necessary to become first-class at any game. He was fond of shooting, but I doubt if he would have enjoyed a covert shoot where a big bag was expected. In his letters describing shooting trips, far more space is devoted to describing the country, the trees, the flowers, the colours, and the people than to details of the sport. I doubt if the size of the bag was ever more than of passing interest to him. A day's shooting gave an opportunity of spending a day with good companions in the open air, striding over new country, seeing new sights and hearing new sounds, making friends with men and women who gather in the crops; and these were the things that satisfied him.

I have referred to his keen interest in naval education, but his interest extended far beyond that limited field, and when his brother was Minister of Education, he took every opportunity of pressing on him his views on national education. His letters to the "P.C.", as he called his brother, were always written in his vivid and compelling style:

. . . I'll give you my views on some aspects of Education — gratis. Quite pleasant to fire off some ammunition at the very Head.

I noted some very sane remarks on Recreation spaces. Good.

Discipline, precision, smartness can only be effected in "an open space"! Nothing of the sort can be done in a classroom. Banging of lids on desks, standing up, sitting down, opening copy-books, all together is damned nonsense & harmful.

But drill in the open, My Crikey you can do a lot of good there. Young bodies erect, chests out, faces clean — there's the good citizen in the making. Go for that part of the business like Hell. Teach self-respect from the very start. Don't cram the little toddlers of 5. Give them games and amusements and bright things to do. Don't teach anything till 7 or 8, except the ordinary virtues of which Discipline is the greatest, and unselfishness probably the next.

By the bye, *do* you get *all* the children (14-15) in from Elementary Schools? In the East End for instance. If not, why not? Register not sufficient? A child of 7 seen in the gutter at 10 A.M. on a Tuesday should be an object of investigation. — Is it?

As regards the Curriculum, of course, that must vary for

the different ages and social grades, but I'm inclined to think, in view of the immense industrial efforts the country will have to make after the War, that *every* boy irrespective of class should put in 6 months at some hard manual trade, if only to make him sympathetic to those whose lives have of necessity to be devoted entirely to it. And about the age of 12 or perhaps earlier in some cases the boy should be given instruction in the meaning of our Empire and its obligation. Not swaggeringly of course. The British as a World influence. Empire a sham unless for the general good & advancement — dependent on every boy & girl — in every walk of life. We must be strong, and always right — strong enough to insist on right conduct *inter*nationally. Men of valour. Women of virtue — Males must be MEN and men trained to defend their rights and the rights of others. Let there be no illusion about Eras of Universal Peace. How can it be in our time. To be weak will be criminal. British invincibly strong with their parliamentary form of Government (which after all is quick to suspect ulterior motives of profit, territory, concession of all sorts) is the greatest guarantee.

Therefore truth, virility & valour and service to the State, and in future be able to trust, not to alliance, but to our own strength. Stories of Great Englishmen should be frequently told — Clive, Hastings, Nicholson, Robt. Scott, Gallipoli landing & all the host of heroes of the War.

These are the sort of thoughts that I expect, survive with difficulty when Routine, Reports, Syllabi, Examinations, Teachers' Salaries, etc. clamour for attention. Also I do see that Inspired Teachers are required, but all the same I fancy our country is expecting not an Educational Measure of "Revised Matters of Instruction" (substituting Applied Science for Dead languages etc.) but one in accord with the great spirit of the moment giving to the people as Tyndall said, "The Knowledge of the Laws by which God's Service is sustained and the perpetual advancement of mankind served. . . ."

His interest in social problems did not stop at education, and I found amongst his papers a strongly worded "Open Letter to the Well-to-do", which he was moved to write at a time when frequent strikes were causing great anxiety, and mistrust between the various grades of our Society. I do not know if it ever left his desk, but I have extracted some passages, as they help to build up his character by revealing his views on the responsibilities of the " well-to-do " to those in less-easy circumstances, and also how he approached his lifelong task and the command of men :

. . . The evil has been one of long & slow growth — so slow that to many its progress has not been manifest. But today we are face-to-face with a situation that should be plain to all and which if grappled with courageously & humanely, instead of marking a stage in the decline of this Empire, may serve as a departure point to greater strength, and wider beneficence than our people has ever yet dreamed of —

. . . You have been ready in the past — You have sadly altered if that is not still the case — Is there any doubt about the urgency today ? Is there any measure of the result, if, for a people divided, mutually suspicious, stumbling forward and quarrelling on the way, you substitute the ordered march of a vast army, united, inter-dependent, fired by common ideals, led to a common goal ?

. . . Remember, Riches and Knowledge are held in trust and it is for their possessors to act up to the terms of the trust.

. . . You, who rush in motor cars through the country, in future make it the rule to help the wayfarer on his road — a bent old man under a heavy load may be, or a tired mother with tired child — How can you pass these ? The sour look of the dust-covered plodder, the careless indifference of the average motorist — all this must cease.

. . . You, to whom History appeals, who glory in the deeds of our forebears, unlock your enthusiasm and set it abroad to fire others ! You, who have not lost reverence, show those who have, how to regain it — reverence for Faith, Virtue, Law — and for The King as the emblem. You, Directors of large industries, be it mine or factory, see to it that every man can work therein retaining his Christian-named identity ; that he is entered, his work appraised and, if necessary, discharged by a responsible unbiassed person, and that the most important factor in all enterprise, the human element, receives justice, assistance, and, above all, interest from someone whom the worker can look up to. This elementary essential to successful handling of men is generally disregarded.

. . . It is incredible that the industrial machine has worked so long on such a crazy basis as the existing one. Are there those who think the " working man " too dull to respond to the call of an ideal? Such have never been to the North. They have not noticed the face full of character & determination, the energy when at work, the thoughtfulness when work is over, the rugged yet poetic form of speech — Poverty is the ally of Nobility — not its enemy — and be it remembered it is only " the dissolute among the rich who speak in opprobrious terms of the follies of the poor."

. . . Now, ladies and gentlemen of position, is the time — the time for action, happy, wholehearted service to your poorer neighbours. There is an imperial call, not to mention a religious call, to all your sons and daughters. Educate & govern, so that every brain may find a director, every hand a helper, every soul a comforter. Take the people to your hearts, trust to their loyalty, lead their labour. If you refuse, hesitate and equivocate, as Ruskin says, " your doom is nearer than ever your adversaries hope and it will be deeper than even your despisers dream ".

I have referred to his love of music and that, too, might have been blunted by years of listening to " Poet and Peasant " on instruments suffering from moist tropical atmosphere and to messmates strumming a piano sadly out of tune.

But it was too much part of him to be killed by the adverse conditions of ship life, and he never missed an opportunity of hearing good music. He would always find time to go to the Opera at Malta. I only found two people for whom he expressed hatred: one was the woman who would talk during *La Traviata*, and the other was an ambitious naval officer who continually intruded when Sir William May was discussing naval policy with Mr. Asquith, then Prime Minister.

His ship's bandmaster must have been rather anxious when he saw him approaching :

Have only this moment come down from the upper deck where the bands have been practising for the Archbishop's visit. Feel very self-satisfied and swaggery. Because they started 166 in the old rub-along-anyhow lifeless way and then I saw in a flash, as I thought, how it ought to go and when they finally played it as I wanted, it made me all gooseflesh with pleasure.

Great sense of *breadth* in that first line. ALL people that on earth — the wide world over — do dwell.

Then that 4th verse — stable as a rock — even — irresistible unchanging time and accent — brushing aside all petty attacks. Last verse — simply *ff*.

It is no surprise that with his early bringing-up he was always a voracious and discriminating reader. Few books of importance escaped him and histories, biographies, and poetry were constantly in the post to meet his insatiable demand for the latest and the best. He would not send back a book that made a special appeal until his friends in the Fleet had had an opportunity of sharing his pleasure in it.

It is, of course, true that Fisher was more fortunate in his early home life and in inherited gifts than most men.

That house in the New Forest, surrounded by open country and woodlands, was a perfect setting for a boy of adventurous and inquiring mind and, then, there was a father who loved the classics and a mother who was a " radiant and heroic spirit who gave to all who came to her for comfort nothing less than her entire heart ", and there were always visitors, who counted for something in public life, and whose conversation was of absorbing interest to a boy eager for knowledge.

At the top of the family tree is that man of striking looks, the Chevalier de L'Etang ; slightly to one side is William Wordsworth ; parallel with the King's tutor are many famous women; parallel with our Fisher are famous names, Darwin, Vaughan Williams, a famous historian and Cabinet Minister, a never-to-be-forgotten tutor of Christ Church.

Yes, he was born under a kindly star; but so have other men who have reaped little benefit, though, unlike Fisher, there has been nothing in their school or university or later life to blunt early interests and enthusiasms.

So that is the man I discovered in the letters, and though there may be some who will say that I have picked out those that suited my purpose of making a portrait without blemish, they will be wrong. If space had permitted, I would gladly have included every one of them.

Let me turn now to his place in history. If history is taken to mean what will be taught in schools to future generations, he may not have a place. History is now on such a vast canvas that the operations of our naval and military forces in a major war, however brilliant, can only be allowed a very small part of the picture.

Our own political history, and the contemporary history of other countries, crowd out events which in any case are not easily understood by the lay mind.

Only an Admiral who has won a decisive victory at sea is remembered and so there are very few of our great sea captains whose names are familiar to the general public, because, unlike armies, fleets take years to build and equip, and even in the longest wars there has seldom been more than one major sea battle between the main fleets. But there will always be students of naval history and those who, not satisfied with the skeleton of naval operations, probe deeper to find out the basic reasons for the success of our arms, and they will not have to probe very far into the history of the First World War before they find the name of the man who brought all his immense energy, his wisdom, his sea experience, and his vision to bear on the baffling problem of reducing the greatest threat to our existence since we had counted as a Power in Europe.

There is, however, another history, and one that will never be written, in which his place is permanent.

Few naval officers in their passage through their service have left such an abiding influence on officers and men who served with them.

From the moment he began to gather strength and stature his shipmates began to feel the influence of his utterly straight, fearless, and generous character.

We have seen the young lieutenant joining a mess that had lost some of the zest and fun of life and the commander joining shipmates in low spirits because their ship could do nothing right and, in a trice, all the cobwebs and gloom giving place to new hope and a new purpose in life.

Wherever he went he brightened the lives of his fellow men, and he must have opened up to hundreds of officers new and exciting fields of thought and endeavour and interest into which they would never have ventured but for him.

And there is something else still more enduring.

Many generations of officers will have joined the Royal Navy, devoted their lives to its service, and given place to the next generation before his methods of training the Fleet for war and his conception of governing the Fleet in peace-time have lost their influence. We have proof already. At Christmas, 1940, Admiral Sir Andrew Cunningham wrote :

> The war progresses slowly out here but everything that has happened has proved how right Sir William was in 1935–1936 during the Abyssinian time. Many a time when confronted with a difficult situation I cast my mind back and ask myself what he would have done, and the answer always comes the same — to take the bold and direct course — and it pays.

Hundreds of young officers are today eagerly watching

how their Admiral plans and conducts his lightning attacks on the enemy and the complex amphibious operations of this fiercest of all maritime wars. So the torch is handed on and they, in their turn, will one day write as Fisher once wrote :

> The Archangel Gabriel is only just good enough for such a Service. For the rest of us, it is only a question of the degree in which we fail to live up to the Navy.